BORN
to the
MOB

The True-Life Story of the Only Man to Work
for All Five of New York's Mafia Families

FRANKIE SAGGIO
AND FRED ROSEN

RUNNING PRESS
PHILADELPHIA • LONDON

Printed in the United States

9   8   7   6   5   4   3
Digit on the right indicates the number of this printing.

Library of Congress Cataloging-in Publication Data is available
ISBN-13: 978-1-56025-559-9
ISBN-10: 1-56025-559-5

Interior design by Paul Paddock

This book may be ordered by mail from the publisher.
Please include $2.50 for postage and handling.
But try your bookstore first!

Running Press Book Publishers
2300 Chestnut Street
Philadelphia, PA 19103-4371

Visit us on the web!
www.runningpress.com

Dedication

For my wife, my one and only true love. Without her I'd not be alive today; she is the most caring person I've ever known. For my father and Uncle Philly, who never leave my thoughts and heart. For my son and daughter, who have taught me courage and the meaning of unconditional love. And for Ben and Judy, who will always have my highest respect and love. —F.S.

For my father Murray Rosen, whose stories about his childhood friend Georgie Seitz, a member of Murder, Incorporated, inspired me. —F.R.

CONTENTS

PREFACE

The slight bulge near Frankie Saggio's ankle from the small two-shot over-and-under .38 Derringer hardly spoiled the razor-sharp crease of his Versace jeans. A black Polo pullover and a belt with a large silver buckle completed his ensemble. We were sitting in the Marriott Hotel in the New Jersey Meadowlands, about sixty miles away from his hideout on Long Island.

During the next few hours we talked about his life in the Mob. At first I didn't believe any of it; it was all too fantastic to be true. In my line of work as a crime journalist, you encounter a lot of people who lie. But careful checking proved an amazing thing: Frankie Saggio was telling the truth.

Over the next two years, we met many times in person while he was being "protected" by the FBI and the U.S. Marshals Service prior to, during, and after his entry into the Federal Witness Security Program. How Frankie came to be a fugitive from the Mob and later from the government, is a story that spans four generations and two continents, from a little village in Italy called Castellammare del Golfo in the 1920s, to New York City on September 11, 2001 and beyond.

To protect lives, some names and locations have been changed. Everything else is true.

—Fred Rosen

"We're a big, rough, rich, wild people and crime is the price we pay for it, and organized crime is the price we pay for organization."
—Philip Marlowe in Raymond Chandler's *The Long Goodbye*

PROLOGUE

"The sound of the shots seemed to echo in my head forever."

Buddy, I remember things by the car I was driving at the time," says Frankie Saggio.

"I used to change cars like most guys change underwear. That night, I had my '99 Dodge Durango parked at my building on the East Side. That's why I was waiting for a cab downtown in the Village. I had just had dinner and drinks and was standing on the curb.

"I took my cigarettes out of my jacket and I was looking for my lighter when I noticed a Caddy double-parked, running, with the windows open. And it's January. What was a car doing with its windows open in *January?* The car starts creepin' down the block. All of a sudden, the engine revs up. As it's passin' under the streetlights, I can see a guy hangin' out the back window and he's got a pistol in each hand.

"I turned. As I did, I could hear the shots, the sound of glass shattering, people screaming, and bullets rippin' past the side of my head. I ran down the stairs and through the restaurant, out the back kitchen door, up the steps, and onto 13th Street. I must have run at least seven or eight blocks, then jumped into a taxi. The sound of the shots seemed to echo in my head forever.

"The first thing I thought of was my wife Aria, who I was separated from at the time. She was at home with her cousin Marie at our house on Long Island. I called my Uncle Sal and told him to get over there and get her out.

"Then I made the taxi driver pass my building to see if anyone was hanging around outside; I needed to get the guns I kept in my apartment. He dropped me off two blocks away. I went through the alley and into the basement where it's pitch black; my mind is racing and I'm trying to think clearly. As I was walking down the hall, my body felt numb, my ears are ringing. My hand shook when I put the key in the lock. I came through the door and dropped facedown: my living room was floor-to-ceiling windows facing 37th Street.

"I crawled on my stomach into the bedroom. It felt like I was gonna get shot any second, heart fucking racing, I grabbed my guns and crawled back into the kitchen and sat on the floor. I heard myself breathing; it sounded so loud, I thought everyone in the building could hear it.

"I figured it had to be Tommy D who wanted me dead. He was my skipper and him and me had had words. I settled down to wait till the sun came up, to see if one of the boys from the crew was going to come and try and finish the job.

"While I waited I remembered how my Uncle Philly made Tommy dress up as Santa when I was a kid. The night never seemed to end. All I kept thinking was, 'I can't believe Santa Claus is trying to kill me.'"

Before the attempt on his life outside Marilou's restaurant on West 12th Street on January 4, 2000, Frankie Saggio was one of the most successful gangsters in the history of the New York City Mob and the only one who commanded respect from all Five Mafia Families. Astoundingly, he achieved that profile without his activities making a line in the newspapers or a sound byte on the news.

Frankie's looks are reminiscent of a Roman Centurion's: chiseled cheekbones, aquiline nose, dark eyes, and a full head of wavy dark hair. But unlike a Centurion that served Caesar, Frankie Saggio served himself. He knew how to use his looks, charm, and viciousness to make money. Whether you belonged to the Lucchese, Columbo, Genovese, Bonanno, or Gambino Family, you knew Frankie because he made money like he printed it. That talent allowed him to do what no one ever had: cross Mob family lines and do business with members of all Five Families, not just his own.

Though he was born into the Bonanno family, Frankie spent much of his time in organized crime as an independent. More than any contemporary gangster, he mastered the one principle necessary for trust and survival: It's all about money. In the modern Mafia, the ability to make money—being an earner—is admired more than loyalty and honor.

Throughout the 1990s, the Mob engaged in a sophisticated form of extortion. Using legitimate, Mob-infiltrated brokerages, members of organized crime used "pump and dump" scams to fleece investors of billions of dollars. They would artificially pump or drive the price of a stock up after its IPO (initial public offering), then dump or sell it when the stock sold at its top price. The stock would then plummet. Legitimate investors had to stay in for fear of losing big. Chief among this shady group was Jarrett Securities, Stratton Oakmont, and Robert Todd Securities, and at one time or another, Frankie Saggio ran all of these firms. Frankie also figured out how to make the money clean by getting a venerable American investing firm to help him out.

"When we sold our customers, we told them their money was safe because a hundred-year-old firm was our partner," Frankie recalls. "Bear Sterns was our clearinghouse. They never asked why our firms kept going in and out of business. They were happy to take our money."

His success in the business was almost a given. For two decades, from the age of sixteen, thirty-seven-year-old Frankie Saggio had been privy to all the Mob deals and murders. He was not some gumba come lately; rather, he had a pedigree few possess. Frankie Saggio was fourth-generation Mafia.

On his mother's side, Frankie's great uncle Suvio Grimaldi was a Mafioso in good standing. On his father's side, his great uncle Jimmy Clemenza (a.k.a. Jimmy Brown) had been a bootlegger with Al Capone in Prohibition-era Chicago. Clemenza would later become a top assassin for the Profaci/Columbo Family. But it was Frankie's uncle on his father's side, Philip "Philly Lucky" Giaccone, who commanded universal respect.

Because of his courtly manners, honest nature, and ability to temper those qualities with brutal ruthlessness when he had to, Philly Lucky was the most respected man in the Mob. He was also a skipper and the heir apparent to the Bonanno Family throne. Even the cops liked him because he never rubbed their noses in his criminal success. But to Frankie, he was "Uncle Philly."

It was Frankie's uncles who tutored him in the ways of the Mob. They raised him to have old-fashioned values of honor and respect and they taught him to behave and dress in accordance with Mafia tradition. For instance, Frankie learned that a Mafioso never wears green because it is a sign of envy. He also learned to always be clean-shaven, with no mustache, as facial hair was a reminder of the crass "Mustache Petes" that ran the Mob three generations back. His uncles taught him that to be a "made" guy, fully accepted into the old Sicilian brotherhood, you had to be of pure Italian blood that flowed through several generations.

It was also Frankie's uncles who taught him the value of a dollar and how to steal it from someone else. They told him to think of himself as a white-collar guy in a blue-collar business. Finally, it was his uncles who taught him how to keep his home life separate from business. To this day, Frankie's teenage daughter Mary, from his first marriage to Anna Gambino, knows nothing about his crimes.

"My uncles were alive and they schooled me. They taught me the business, the right way to do things," Frankie says.

Frankie Saggio believed that all men in the Mob were like his uncles and always would be. Frankie should have been a boss himself, like his "Uncle Philly," and he had everything in place to achieve just that. But it all came crashing down when those shots were fired from the back window of the Caddy on West 12th Street. Clutching his guns in his apartment that night, waiting for guys from his own crew to come and finish the job, to kill him on capo Tommy D's orders, Frankie thought about his life. From the time he was a kid, he had been in the life.

Frankie Saggio had been born to the Mob.

PART ONE:
THE OUTFIT

Chapter One
LEARNING TO DRIVE

Philip Giaccone was born in the Ridgewood neighborhood of Brooklyn. Giaccone's father died when he was young, leaving him, his sister, and his mother to figure out how to survive in the midst of the Great Depression.

"My uncle carried a picture in his wallet. It was of him as a kid, maybe two or three, dressed in rags. He would tell everybody, 'See, that's me on Gratin Street.' Gratin Street was the street with the poorest people in Brooklyn and Uncle Philly, well, he was pretty poor," says Frankie.

John Bonaventre ran the rackets in the neighborhood for the Bonanno Family and he took a liking to young Giaccone. He watched as the boy went through junior high and high school, getting nineties and hundreds in his math courses, noting the kid really had a head for figures and business. And he came from good stock. Bonaventre and Phil's mom both came from Castellammare del Golfo. For an Italian who might be seeking entry to the Mob, that was something special.

Castellammare del Golfo is a small fishing village on the island of Sicily, forty miles west of Palermo. Most of the original members of the Bonanno Crime Family were Castellammarese. With Giaccone's Castellammarese pedigree, Bonaventre thought he'd make a good soldier and recruited him into the Family. But Giaccone was too smart for that; he knew that if he became involved, he would die an untimely death. He was well aware of Mafia history and was determined not to be a part of it.

Giaccone knew that the Mob was brilliant in its organization along family lines, with each family named after its founder: Lucchese for

Frank Lucchese, Genovese for Vito Genovese, Bonanno for Joseph Bonanno, Gambino for Carlo Gambino, and Profaci for Joe Profaci. The Mafia was actually the inner circle of each of these families, composed of made men.

To become a made member of the Mafia, you had to be one-hundred percent Italian. For an Italian male with criminal aspirations, intermarriage robbed him of the opportunity to become a made guy. Within the wiseguy life, being made wasn't only a badge of honor; more importantly, it meant keeping a bigger share of the criminal spoils.

Bottom line: Being in the Mob was a dangerous line of work with a high mortality rate. There was only one way out of working for any of those guys: feet first.

Giaccone tried hard to make a legitimate go of it, but the Depression saw unemployment climb to twenty-five percent. Options were few. Even the odd jobs he could find never lasted long. There was something in his personality that demanded more action, more money. So when Bonaventre came back a second time, Giaccone signed up.

Philip "Philly Lucky" Giaccone didn't look like the movie version of a gangster (think DeNiro, Brando, or even Cagney); he was quiet and well mannered, described by all as a gentleman and a man of his word.

During Giaccone's first two decades in the life, from the late 1930s to the late 1950s, J. Edgar Hoover's FBI never acknowledged that the Mob even existed. To do so would have been to admit that there existed a vast criminal conspiracy based upon an ancient Italian society, and that the organization trafficked in violence. The Feds would actually have to do something to fight it, which they didn't. Faced with what was literally a license to steal, the Mob responded with greed.

A series of assassinations fractured the peace among the Five Families. Finally, in 1957, the bosses—Tommy Lucchese, Vito Genovese, Joseph Bonanno, Carlo Gambino, and Joe Profaci—decided to get together and hash things out to restore an accord. The place they picked was the house of a man named Joseph Barbara in the upstate town of Apalachin. It was a rural location, where they figured they'd be safe from prying eyes.

• • •

NOVEMBER 13, 1957

"My uncle told me the story of how he gets this phone call. The guy on the other end of the line was his skipper, John Bonaventre. Bonaventre told my uncle to pack a bag. He was about to take a trip to upstate New York to guard the boss, Joe Bonanno. Bonanno was going to some sort of meeting," recounts Frankie.

The next day, Giaccone rode with Bonanno in a sedan up the Hutchinson River Parkway, into the lower Hudson Valley. When they got to Barbara's place in Apalachin, the bosses went inside to meet, confident they were free from scrutiny. Left outside was their contingent of chauffeurs and bodyguards, over fifty armed men in all. Driving past in a black and white cruiser were New York State Police Sergeant Edward Croswell and Trooper Vincent Vasisko. Eyeing the suspicious looking men, some of whom were roaming the Barbara property with shotguns, they radioed in for reinforcements.

The house was surrounded. The cops raided the meeting. A few guys, including Philip Giaccone and John Bonaventre, managed to escape capture by getting lost in the woods that encircled the Barbara property.

Frankie remembers how Philly Lucky described his escape. "Uncle Philly told me that he found his way back to the road. He ran into Bonaventre who told him to come with him. Bonaventre drove to a farmhouse nearby, opened up the door and showed him what was inside. Bonaventre had kidnapped a state trooper, then handcuffed and gagged him. Bonaventre figured to use him as a hostage in case the cops closed in on them.

"'John, I think you should let him go. They got nothing on us. We'd actually have a kidnap beef. Let's get the hell out of here while we still can,' Uncle Philly told Bonaventre. And that's what happened. They stole a car, drove down some deserted road, threw the guy, unharmed, out of the car and drove back to the city like nothing happened."

On the surface, nothing significant appeared to have happened; none of the bosses had any outstanding warrants. They were all freed within hours of their arrests. But the fact of their existence had finally been proven. Hoover and the FBI could no longer deny that the Mob existed. They had no choice left but to fight.

The Outfit was out of the shadows. Philip Giaccone knew that would make business a little more difficult. For him, though, Apalachin brought to light the Faustian bargain he had accepted years before with John Bonaventre's offer of "employment." Giaccone gave the Bonanno Family his allegiance. In return, the Bonannos supplied a Depression kid with a good living. But he was too much of a Catholic to do what most soldiers in the Outfit had done. He would not, under any circumstances, give up his soul.

How could his family respect him if he was forever labeled in the newspaper as "suspected Mafia member"? What would have happened had he been arrested at Apalachin? He knew better than to rely on the guys he would be forced to do business with. How could he provide for his family if he was arrested and served time in jail?

The answer was simple: he wouldn't be labeled, he wouldn't be suspected, he wouldn't be arrested, and he wouldn't go to jail. *Ever.* Philip Giaccone had so much personal honor, he could never imagine such an eventuality, despite being a mob skipper.

SEPTEMBER 7, 1964

From the early part of the twentieth century, many Castellammarese had settled in the Bensonhurst neighborhood of Brooklyn. It was in Bensonhurst, on September 7, 1964, that seventeen-year-old Petrina Caliazzo gave birth to her son. She and her husband Dennis Saggio named him Frank. Almost immediately, everyone started calling the baby "Frankie."

Frankie grew up in an all-brick, two-family attached house at 6717 17th Avenue, a two-way street lined with elm trees. In Frankie's Bensonhurst neighborhood (or "Benzinhoist," as the residents pronounced it with their Brooklyn accents), you could still get a fresh-baked bagel at midnight any day of the week at the bagel shop on the corner of 66th Street and 17th Avenue. A little further down on 18th Avenue at 66th Street, there was an Italian bakery that had the sweetest, creamiest cannoli.

Few people had air conditioning in those days. In summer, you sat out on the stoop, the concrete steps that led up to your house, and were cooled by the breeze coming in off the Narrows. Frankie Saggio was a smart boy. On those nights when he sat out with his uncles Philly and

Jimmy, he listened. Frankie listened right on through his childhood, down oh 18th Avenue, the neighborhood's main street for shopping and socializing, where he played in front of the social clubs that fronted for Mafia crews, where cops on the pad stopped in for their weekly taste. It was a neighborhood where no one did or said anything serious without first getting approval from one of the heads of New York's Five Families.

"The wiseguys, to me they were the captains of industry," says Frankie "After school, I used to play outside the social clubs on 18th Avenue and watch them go in and out. My dad owned an auto body shop and also had a no-show job at Kennedy Airport. My whole family worked there. Uncle Philly controlled the rackets out at JFK Airport for the Bonannos. We took everything possible out of that airport.

"People would joke around and say it was stuff that had fallen off the truck. Fallen off the truck—hell! We opened the containers and took what we wanted. It was the price of doing business at Kennedy Airport. Growing up we had all kinds of boxes of stuff around.

"One time, I walked into our living room and my uncles Philly, Jimmy, Carl, and Satch—every one of them had the same suit. They had robbed a truck full of suits. Another time, they robbed a truck that was supposed to be full of watches, but it turned out to be wigs. I remember my Uncle Satch telling me that he and my Uncle Philly had robbed a trailer. We actually built, like, a makeshift warehouse in two days to unload it.

"My dad Dennis, he didn't get involved in that stuff. My dad he had hemophilia. He had to go in and out of the hospital for transfusions. Between that and his work, he wasn't around a lot. My mom, Petrina, she was a housewife. She had me when she was just seventeen. And she had to handle me and my sister Lina and my dad's illness. It was a lot. So my Uncle Philly, he took up the slack. When I started school he told me, 'Frankie, if someone bothers you in school or on the street, you pick up anything you find—a baseball bat, a brick, a garbage can—and bash their skull in.'

"My uncle first started taking me to 'sit-downs' across the river in Little Italy when I was seven years old and then we'd go get a haircut and shoeshine and lunch at Umberto's or Matty the Horse's joint or Lefty Ruggiero's. Lefty had a joint before he was even a made guy. Lefty was supposed to be made but because he was a gambler, he had to pay back his gambling debts before they would make him.

"'You want to be made? Give us the 50Gs you owe us and you'll get made,' they told him. Lefty didn't get it. He wasn't one of the brightest guys around.

"'See Frankie,' my uncle always said, 'don't ever gamble; you run the games and never be a player—the house always wins.' My Uncle Philly knew what he was talking about. He had a couple of horse rooms and a tremendous shylock business."

On New Year's Day, 1966, John Lindsay became the first Republican to be elected mayor of New York City since Fiorello La Guardia in 1940. The city began to erode.

It was Lindsay who capitulated to the unions and gave them huge contracts. It was Lindsay who was soft on crime. It was Lindsay whose two administrations saw the welfare rolls soar. Lindsay left the city almost financially and morally bankrupt when he stepped down in 1974.

The Saggio and Giaccone families decided it would be better to raise their kids on Long Island. They pulled up stakes and headed east on the Belt Parkway, passing the wetlands that the federal government had laughingly titled "The Gateway National Recreation Area." Being marshy, it actually made a great place for wiseguys to dump a body, which happened every now and then.

After passing JFK, the road curved south, becoming the Southern State Parkway. Then you were on Long Island, the island of privilege. For those living in Brooklyn, it was the "Promised Land" of postage stamp–sized lots with detached houses. The Saggios moved to the mid-Island working class suburb of Deer Park. The Giaccones settled on the rich north shore in Dix Hills.

"Uncle Philly owned a palace in Dix Hills. I was at my uncle's all the time," says Frankie. "Me and Philip [Giaccone Jr.] were like brothers. I really lived there. It was a real neighborhood, a lot like Brooklyn. Anna Gambino lived next door. Anna, she was beautiful. I really liked her. And she had a sister as pretty as she was. Philip liked her and we used to double date. Her father was a cousin of Carlo Gambino, but he was strictly legitimate. He had come from Italy and made a lot of money in the marble and granite business."

The Giaccone's mansion had not one but two kitchens, custom-made French provincial furniture through all the rooms, and the entire interior was gilded in marble, right out to the small marble stoop up to the front door. Outside in the garden was a gazebo, and a bit further on was an in-ground pool with cabanas. For protection and privacy, Giaccone hired artisans to construct a big stone wall around the whole house, but nothing kept the cops out.

Philly Lucky's suspected criminal activities had gotten him some unwanted attention from the federal and state cops. Sometimes they'd stake out his new house in Dix Hills to see if anything was happening. Of course, nothing ever was. The cops took to identifying his big white colonial as "The White House."

Phil Giaccone had good relations with law enforcement. The cops respected him because he was from the old school. He knew they had a job to do. He never gave them any shit, unlike punks such as one John Gotti, whom Giaccone couldn't stand. Gotti didn't give the cops a shred of respect, which is why they were always on him. Giaccone, on the other hand, was always polite. Maybe he couldn't get the cops on his side—the ones who weren't on the take, that is—but there was value in having them respect him.

"He had a garage filled with cases of lobster, filet mignon, shrimp—anything you wanted. You had to stay by him a week for Christmas. 'You want to go home? What's wrong with you?' he'd ask anyone who wanted to leave early. Those were the best days," reminisces Frankie's mother, Petrina Saggio.

"When my brother-in-law was around, no one wanted for anything. Christmas was a fairy tale, like nothing I ever saw. Santa Claus was there. Phil'd [sic] buy all the kids bikes. Me, Frankie, and his cousin Philip got motorcycles. His daughter Corinne got a new Mercedes convertible one year, mink coats too. Phil rented a bus so everyone could go chop down a Christmas tree."

Frankie's sister Lina remembers, "We were always together—sisters and brothers and kids. Phil rented a camper and took us all to Lake

George in the summer. I was the only girl. My father didn't want us to go. 'I'll take care of her—don't worry about it,' Uncle Phil told my dad. He made me sleep in bus with him so he could watch me and make sure nothing happened."

Giaccone had mastered the essential element that allowed him to enjoy the spoils of his criminal life without ever looking over his shoulder for the cops: "Uncle Philly" was one guy and "Philly Lucky" was another.

"Uncle Philly always came home for dinner by 6 P.M. every night he was alive. If a member of Philly Lucky's crew came to his house with a girlfriend, Uncle Philly would answer the door and tell him, 'You bring your wife or you don't come,' and he would close the door in the guy's face," says Frankie.

About the business end of things Frankie remembers, "Uncle Philly was always getting envelopes from guys. Every captain has a taste of the business of every guy in his crew. One time we were playing in the snow and there's an envelope in this ski jacket and on it is written 25K. I brought it in the house.

"'Uncle Philly,' I said, 'you left this in the jacket pocket.'

"'My God, I forgot all about this,' Uncle Philly said, and he laughed. I figured that was the only way to make money—to get it in envelopes from guys or to steal it. He was a man of his word."

Indeed he was. Philly Lucky was never arrested. Not once. Among the Five New York Families, no one had ever attained the rank of capo, one rung below boss, without ever being officially accused by law enforcement. And that's how Philip Giaccone became "Philly Lucky," the only straight-arrow member of the Mob who didn't drink, womanize, or get arrested. Behind his back, his men who loved him called him "The Priest."

"I really wanted to be like my uncle," says Frankie.

In 1979, Frankie really began following in his uncle's footsteps. He committed his first felony. He was all of fifteen years old.

"Me and my cousin Philip, my Uncle Philly's son, went and robbed some fireworks and money," Frankie recalls. "We knew the guy who sold the stuff and where he lived. We broke the window of his house, got in, and took the stuff. I got out first, and then when I looked back, Philip had been caught. Some guy from next door had grabbed him and called the owner.

"I don't know what to do so I go back to my aunt and uncle's and I'm waiting. We're sitting down to dinner. My cousin Peter was there too. Peter was about to marry my cousin Corinne, Philly's daughter. Anyway, I haven't said a word and the phone rings."

Philip was on the phone.

"'Mom,' he tells my Aunt Annette, 'I'm over at so and so's house down the block and they're accusing me of trying to break into the place.' My Uncle Philly, he turns to Peter and pulls a wad of cash from his pocket.

"'Peter, take this and give the guy whatever he wants. Take Frankie with you.' On the way over, I tell Peter what happened. 'Don't worry Frankie,' he said.

"When we get there, Peter schmoozes the guy whose house we broke into. After fifteen minutes, he hands the guy some cash and Philip walks away with us. No charges, no nothin'. When we got home, Peter explained to my uncle what had happened.

"'Which one of you did it?' Uncle Philly asked us.

"He took us both in the bedroom one at a time and questioned us. Philip didn't tell him anything. Me neither. Uncle Philly was kind of mad that we wouldn't confide in him. But he was also really happy that we kept our mouths shut.

"'Never be a stool pigeon, Frankie,' he said."

Chapter Two
RALLY SPORTS CORVETTE

The summer of 1979 was the summer that Peter Clemenza (son of the Columbo skipper Jimmy Clemenza) and Corinne Giaccone (daughter of the Bonanno skipper) were getting married. Their wedding was "the talk of all Long Island because the offspring of two Mob families were uniting in marriage," remembers Frankie's mother, Petrina Saggio. "The wedding was two years in the planning. It was going to take place at The Sands in Long Beach, a fancy place on the south shore of Long Island. We all went downtown and got dresses: me, Annette, my daughter Lina, and, of course, Corinne."

That same summer, Philly Lucky was getting a lot of agita.

"Uncle Philly had this business, Pinto Trucking, a nationwide trucking outfit that he ran with my Uncle Carl," Frankie says. "This was in addition to the rackets my uncle controlled at the airport for the Bonannos. One day, a guy on my Uncle Philly's crew—Tommy DiFiore, who we called Tommy D—starts an argument with my Uncle Carl. I was in the office helping out.

"'Carl,' Tommy D says to my uncle, 'You're the manager of the office and the phones suck. They don't work, you fucking asshole,' he's screamin' and cursin'.

"'It's the phone company. I'm working on gettin' it fixed,' my Uncle Carl explained. Well, my Uncle Philly walks in and hears what's going on.

"'Who do you think you're talking to—you insult my family?'

"Now Philly's yellin' at Tommy D. Before Tommy could say anything, my uncle grabs him by the throat and he takes off, trying to get away. And my uncle corners the muthafucker in the warehouse out back. It's dark and Uncle Philly is in a fucking rage.

"'Don't show your face in this office again. You ever come around, you'll end up rolled up in a carpet.'"

Tommy D was banished from Philly Lucky's crew, which left a vacancy. But before Philly Lucky had a chance to fill it, still another problem came up. A struggle for power had developed in the Bonanno Family. On one side was the defacto boss, Rusty Rastelli, who was away in an upstate prison. His arch-rival, Carmine Galante, was trying to butch in on his action.

"When my Aunt Annette sat down in July to make out the invitations for the September wedding, Uncle Philly told her to hold off on putting Galante's name down. I was just a kid, but I knew something was up. I had been to enough sit-downs with my Uncle Philly and ate many lunches with the man I called 'Uncle Carmine.' Something wasn't right. I thought they were real tight."

The FBI file on Carmine Galante numbers over two thousand pages and spans five decades, from the 1930s through the 1970s. A contemporary of Lucky Luciano, Galante was one of the most well-known and feared gangsters. Short and stocky, Carmine Galante was born in Harlem in 1910 of Castellammarese parents. A lifelong criminal, he loved cigars. From that habit came his nickname, Lillo, for "little cigar."

Galante was first arrested at the age of fourteen in 1924 for petty theft, then graduated to the more grown-up crimes of grand larceny, robbery, and assault over the next two years. On December 25, 1930, when he was twenty years old, he got into a running gun battle with a cop in the Williamsburg neighborhood of Brooklyn while escaping from the Liebman Brewery in South Brooklyn where he'd just committed an armed robbery. A six-year-old girl on the street with her mother, was shot and wounded during the shoot-out. Galante was captured, found guilty of armed robbery, and sent up the Hudson River to the port town of Ossining, where he was housed for eight years at the infamous Sing Sing Prison.

After his release, Galante became a made man in the Bonanno Family by assassinating Italian anarchist/social activist Carlo Testa in 1942.

Over the next twenty-five years, he worked his way up the ladder to become the East Coast's largest drug supplier. With Joe Bonanno pushed out as family head in the late 1960s, and new boss Philip "Rusty" Rastelli convicted in April 1976 on federal racketeering charges, Galante began solidifying power.

Galante supplied more heroin to the United States than any other gangster. His zips—the young, tough Sicilian Mafioso who earned their nickname because they talked fast, or "zipped" through the language—were his muscle. And he was the Mob's premium earner. It all looked good for Frankie's Uncle Carmine to take over. But Uncle Carmine had made one mistake.

To the Five Families, drugs were the kiss of death. For as much money as the fruit of the poppy brought in, the deadly plant and its heroin derivative brought even more public outcry for a ban on its importation. As a result, involvement with drugs meant that the Mob found itself under excessive federal scrutiny. Since organized crime thrives on secrecy, the Five Families began having difficulty conducting their more acceptable businesses like gambling, loan sharking, and prostitution. The Commission met and gave their approval for a solution to the problem.

The Commission is the Mafia's regulatory body, composed of the bosses of all Five Families. All major disputes between families are brought to the Commission. Only the Commission can sign off on an assassination of a made guy; protocol calls for it not to be done by the individual who holds the grudge. That individual first has to bring the grievance to the Commission, which then rules on it. Unfortunately for Carmine, the Commission decided that he had to go.

Frankie recalls the day it happened. "It was on my father's birthday, July 12, 1979. We were over at my Uncle Philly's in Dix Hills for a barbecue. My uncle got a phone call. Uncle Philly listened for about a minute, just nodding and whispering a few words.

"'Carmine is dead,' he said after hanging up. Then he started to explain what had happened."

Three hours earlier, just before noon in the Bushwick neighborhood of Brooklyn, Carmine Galante got out of his chauffeur-driven Lincoln limousine in front of his favorite neighborhood restaurant, Joe and Mary's. Lillo was smoking a cigar. He wore a white, short-sleeved shirt and blue slacks. In his pockets were social security and Medicaid cards and $2,860 in cash. (Gangsters always carry a lot of cash—who would be stupid enough to rob them?)

Galante said goodbye to his driver and walked inside. He was shown to his regular table in the rear, next to the patio, where he sat down to a lunch of salad, fish, and red wine. His back was to the patio door. After the meal, Lillo lit up again and settled back for a good smoke. Two of his zips came in and joined him.

At about 2:45 P.M., the door to the restaurant opened. The three men who entered were armed and masked. They made their way quickly to the rear. It seemed like the middle guy's double-barreled shotgun got there before he did.

Just as Galante was rising, thirty pellets of razor-sharp buckshot ripped into his chest. A second shotgun blast took away the left side of his face. The other two gunmen took care of the bodyguards, killing them instantly, then turned their sights on Galante again.

That he was already dead didn't matter. The goal was to leave a message for any guys who thought they were bigger than the Outfit. The assassin with the double barrel fired again into Galante's back. The blast resonated as far east as Dix Hills, in the home of Philly Lucky. Frankie and his uncle discussed who had clipped Carmine. The identity of the murderers has always remained a well-guarded Mob secret. Until now.

"'It was Whack Whack, Caesar, and Baldo that done it,' my uncle told me. Whack Whack [Anthony] Indelicato was a good friend of mine. He was the son of Sonny Red Indelicato, the capo that was partners with my uncle. Caesar Bonaventre, he was in his twenties, the youngest capo in Mob history and the nephew of my uncle's old boss John Bonaventre. And Baldo Amato—a real tough soldier—he and Caesar were cousins. They'd grown up together in Castellammare del Golfo."

The night Galante was assassinated, Frankie stayed at The White House. Early the next morning, Uncle Philly woke his twelve-year-old nephew.

"'C'mon Frankie,' he said. 'We're taking a ride.' I asked my uncle where we were going and he said, 'Vets Highway and the LIE Exit 57.' There was a hotel out there where my uncle would meet Sonny Red all the time."

Phil Giaccone tooled his Caddy down the off-ramp of the Long Island Expressway, took a left over the bridge spanning the always-congested LIE and stopped in the parking lot of the Red Roof Inn on the right. Another car was already there, waiting. When the occupants saw Philly Lucky get out of his car with his nephew Frankie and son Philip, they came over to kiss and shake hands.

"There was Sonny Red, Anthony Bruno, Dominic Trinchero, and these two zips," Frankie recalls. "The reason for the meeting was to talk about dividing up Carmine's territory and who would take power."

What Frankie didn't know until much later was that with Rastelli in prison and Galante out of the way, Philly Lucky was being "nominated" by those same three capos to take over as boss.

The time had finally come for the golden event of the Mob social season: the marriage of Peter Clemenza and Corinne Giaccone.

"I used to spend a lot of time with Corinne," says Frankie's sister, Lina Saggio. "I was the kid cousin. We were like sisters. The night before she got married we hung out together because I was one of the bridesmaids. The next morning, Corinne got dressed in a beautiful Dior gown that cost about eighteen thousand. Then in come these makeup artists and hairdressers to do up the bride and all the bridesmaids.

"When we walked outside, I couldn't believe what I was seeing: twenty-two limos, each looking like they stretched a block, lined up in front of The White House. It was great, a lot of fun. I thought I was a movie star. Everything was always extravagant with that family."

Everyone drove over to St. Matthew's Roman Catholic Church in Dix Hills. And the wedding began. Following the wedding contingent, the bride's parents walked her down the aisle.

"'You sure you don't want to change your mind? I don't care how much money I spent,' I heard Uncle Phil say to Corinne," Lina recalls. "My uncle thought no man was good enough for her."

Afterward, "there were all these limos outside. Millions of flowers. It was a Saturday night in September, a beautiful night. We went to The Sands. As we entered the hall, there were roses three-feet high—twelve dozen of them in vases all over the place. Carved ice castles, strolling violin players, and harp players. Mounds of fresh salmon, lobster, shrimp, and caviar. Waiters coming around with cigarettes and cigars. Carving tables with every kind of meat.

"There were three rooms going at once. One was a disco, one was oldies, and one had a light show and bubbles. The main room had a full orchestra. When you went to order dinner, there was a complete menu: filet mignon, lobster—whatever you wanted.

"Since I was in the wedding party, I sat on the dais. It was the beginning of the home video era and my uncle had gotten these guys to tape the wedding with this huge Betamax. You know, where they ask people to say a few words to the happy couple? What I could never figure out is why Sally Farrugia, Stevie Cannone, Sonny Napolitano, Joey Massino, Paul Castellano, Carmine Persico, John Gotti, Sammy Gravano—all these guys that were there as guests, kept pushing the mikes and cameras away! Why didn't they want to be taped saying a nice word to the bride and groom?"

Lina's naïveté was understandable.

"Girls didn't know much and my brother he knew *everything*," she says.

Not everything. What Frankie didn't know until later was that Rusty Rastelli was not about to let Phil Giaccone take over as boss. From prison, he put out the word to clip Giaccone and the capos that supported him. And supporting him were all those mobsters at Corinne's wedding who didn't want themselves on tape wishing Philly Lucky's kid well.

During the day, Philly Lucky could usually be found at one of two places: Kennedy Airport where he controlled the rackets for the Bonanno Family, or at his place on nearby Rockaway Boulevard where he had his legitimate business, Pinto Trucking, that fronted for his criminal enterprises.

"'See Frankie,' my uncle told me, 'you be a big earner. Remember the guys above you get ten percent of everything you make.'"

Frankie wanted to be a big earner who'd get his money in

envelopes from others guys. But to do that, he needed a start. In 1980, Frankie dropped out of high school and began to hang with his Uncle Philly's crew.

The Giaccone crew headquarters was "along this weeded marshland that surrounded the Belt Parkway at Kennedy Airport," Frankie remembers. "At a loading dock in the back of a block-long warehouse, tightly secured by an eight-foot barbed-wire fence, that's where we met. All the families had guys out at the airport.

"The guy on my uncle's crew I really loved was Carlo Carerra. They used to call him the 'Mad Bomber' because he was an expert with explosives."

Or thought he was.

"Carlo and another guy on my uncle's crew, Fat Chubby, they went to blow up this carting guy for my uncle. Carlo is using a garage door opener to detonate the explosives, which he's secretly placing under this guy's car at his house. Now, he's under the car, setting up the explosives. Fat Chubby's cruisin' the block. He's down the street when he sees the car blow up. Carlo comes running out into the street like he's a log on fire. What had happened was, somebody on the same frequency pressed their garage door opener and it detonated the bomb before Carlo could get away.

"Fat Chubby rushes Carlo to the hospital. He was burned over ninety percent of his body. The cops come. They want to charge Chubby with Carlo's murder—Carlo isn't even dead yet! Well, those fucks were in for a surprise. Carlo's about six-four and two-seventy [height and weight], a real bull. Skin grafts, the whole nine yards, and he survives. But after he recovers, they charge Carlo with trying to blow the guy up."

Philly Lucky always supported his men. But he couldn't take the risk of being tied to Carlo directly.

"'Everyone put up your house to get Carlo out,' my uncle told all my relatives. And that's what happened: my father—everybody—put up their houses to get Carlo out on bail."

Carlo's freedom was short-lived. He was convicted and subsequently went away for twelve years.

The rest of the guys on that crew nicknamed Frankie "Little

Gangster." The name got shortened to "the Gangster" in all the FBI files in which Frankie Saggio's name appears.

Phil though, had as safe and cozy an existence as any mobster could want. And then, one day, the formerly separate lives of Uncle Philly and Philly Lucky finally merged.

MAY 5, 1981

At about 11 A.M., the phone rang at The White House. Seventeen-year-old Frankie Saggio took the call.

"'Tell Philly not to go to the meeting tonight,' this guy said and then the line went dead. The guy didn't say who he was. But I recognized the voice. It was Donnie Brasco, who worked with Lefty Ruggiero. Lefty had brought him into the family."

Frankie ran upstairs to tell his uncle.

"'Frankie,' my uncle says knotting this blue tie, 'I never expected to make fifty.' He was forty-nine at the time. Then the phone rang again. It was Skin Camarada, my uncle's chauffeur and bodyguard.

"'Philly, I don't feel too well; I'm not coming to work today.' Skin, he had a bad heart for thirty years. It was a joke. But he just happened to pick that day to get *really* sick?"

Petrina Saggio was visiting that morning and remembers watching Phil Giaccone come down the stairs. He saw her sitting on the sofa.

"'There's this little dispute with Sonny Red. Some of the guys have a problem so I gotta go with him,' Phil told me," says Petrina. "He knew there was going to be trouble. He knew they were using Sonny to get to him. But still Phil had to go to that meeting. He would *never* leave a friend to go to his death alone. He had to protect his honor as a man. That was more important than his family at home. In that business, you have to think that way. Otherwise, you know you are going to die anyway."

Petrina watched him go.

"Phil wore a shirt and tie, a beautiful custom-fitted sport jacket, and a well-tailored pair of slacks. He was always very well dressed. Beautiful manner, reserved, quiet, courtly."

The Saggio and Giaccone families knew that Philly Lucky was

walking into trouble and that Uncle Philly might not return that night—or ever again. All they could do was hope. Maybe Philly Lucky would live up to his nickname once again.

"Everybody is waiting it out. By 7 P.M., when Phil doesn't come home for dinner, Annette starts calling everybody, panicking. Frankie stayed by the phones all night," says Petrina. But no one called.

"The next day, my father came to school to pick up Frankie, Philip, and me because something had happened," continues Lina. "Everyone whispered that Uncle Philly didn't come home. That's when I put two and two together. I was worried, scared."

By Sunday, Uncle Philly had been missing for three days. The Giaccone and Saggio families were in limbo. But they'd been around long enough to know. There was no way Phil Giaccone wouldn't come home unless . . . But no one voiced their fears. They couldn't be sure. It was an awful position for a family to be in, not knowing if one of their own was dead or alive.

"Then the cops finally called at the end of May. They found my uncle's car someplace in Brooklyn. But he wasn't in it," says Frankie.

At the same time, some kids playing in a vacant lot at Ruby Street and Blake Avenue in Ozone Park, Queens, bent down to look at something strange sticking out of a canvas sack. That "something" was all green and brown, and it smelled. They called their parents to come and have a look. The parents took one sniff and knew.

The odor of a rotting human body is unlike any other. When Frankie picked up the New York *Daily News* on May 28, 1981, he was in for a surprise. The story was in Section B, on page 4, column 4:

Murder Victim In Queens Identified as Crime Figure

by Leonard Buder

A murder victim found in a vacant Queens lot on Sunday was identified as Alphonse Indelicato, a reported capo in the organized crime "family" once headed by Carmine Galante. Mr. Galante was shot to death nearly two years ago.

The article went on to mention the other missing Bonanno men, including "Philip Giaccone, who has been identified by organized crime-experts in the Police Department as the Bonanno organization's adviser."

"The cops figured the rains had washed Sonny Red's body to the surface and the discovery was accidental." Frankie says otherwise. "Bullshit. Nothing in the Outfit happens by accident. It was deliberate. The reason they let the body be discovered is they figured there would be a funeral and that would be a way to get to Anthony [Whack Whack], Sonny Red's son. With Anthony on the street, none of them would be safe. Sonny Black and the other capos who supported Rastelli, they were scared to death of Anthony because he was a nut job. He was fearless."

Whack Whack might have been fearless, but he wasn't insane. He knew Sonny Black had signed his death warrant. He hid out in Hallandale, FL, where he remained safe. While Sonny Red's death had been confirmed, the other two capos were still missing and presumed dead. For Annette Giaccone, that kind of stress was intolerable.

"Annette knew people," says Petrina. "She finds out through the grapevine—for sure now—that Phil had been killed. She took it bad. Annette, she never stopped grieving. Corinne, Phil Jr.—they were beside themselves. They'd lost their father. But Phil had made sure to provide for his family. Annette had a lot of money in the bank from Phil's [legitimate] businesses. That was another reason for the families to want Phil dead, so they could take his illegitimate businesses."

And seventeen-year-old Frankie Saggio?

"I felt confused," Frankie says. "I didn't know what was true and what wasn't. We were kids and no one told us anything. The neighborhood, they were talking about who might have done it lots of B.S. going around. It was a hard time for Philip [Jr.]. We were like brothers, very close. But you know, in all the years from then until now, we never discussed what happened to his father. We never discussed Uncle Philly's death."

More than the grief he felt, the hardest thing for Frankie was figuring out "whodunnit." To pull off that kind of massacre meant a conspiracy.

"You didn't know who was involved and who wasn't. Obviously some were involved and some weren't. Guys from my uncle's crew started coming around, looking to befriend Phillip and me. I didn't know who to trust until guys were suddenly being made guys who'd had no shot before. They were nobodies and all of a sudden, they're being made. The idea was that guys who did something to help kill my uncle, they'd get made afterwards. It was a promise."

One of those guys who got made after Giaccone's death was his chauffeur and bodyguard who'd called in sick: Skin Camarada.

"My uncle saved Skin's life a hundred times!" exclaims an indignant Frankie. "He was a degenerate gambler who couldn't be trusted. Here's a guy no one in their right mind would let get made. Well guess what? Skin got made after my uncle died."

And then who should resurface but Tommy D.

"Amazing, isn't it? Soon as my uncle was out of the way, he was back on the crew. Now I wonder how that happened?"

Tommy was even making nice to Frankie.

Petrina says, "I told my son, 'Are you out of your mind? This guy is going to have it in for you. Never trust him. Uncle Philly threw him out. He's coming around to keep an eye on you and Philip. He probably figures you and Philip want to get revenge, so he'll put you under his wing so you don't kill him and he can keep an eye on you.' Because you got to remember, Frankie and Philip would want revenge. They would have to."

The path Frankie and his cousin Philip were now on was not what it was supposed to be.

Petrina continues. "My brother-in-law had no intention of either of those boys going into this life. He knew how bad it was. With Frankie, we tried discipline, to discourage him. It didn't work. He wasn't a baby. And the wiseguys he was meeting? They weren't like his uncles. He looked up to his uncles and thought the rest were all like that. They are not. Jimmy Clemenza—Jimmy was my mother-in-law's first cousin—he was very honorable. The young guys coming up, they'd started to lose it."

Tommy D was actually from Giaccone's generation, an older gangster in his mid-fifties who had the discipline to keep his name out of the papers.

"Yeah, I had to give him that. He wasn't flashy like the young guys. But he was still an asshole. See, he kept comin' around and I knew it was only a matter of time till I'd finally have to be a full-time member of Tommy's crew."

Things had changed.

"When my uncle was alive, I was the nephew of a captain. You had the respect: you could do pretty much what you wanted, you had the red carpet. Then he's dead and things ain't as easy as they were. All of a sudden a guy who was an asshole before is talking shit. He's now somebody.

"Most of the guys on my uncle's crew loved him, but they needed to make a livin'. They split up. Guys went to different Families. When a boss dies, it's a little easier to do that under the circumstances. There's no one to say you can't do it. We called them fence-jumpers. Guys like Carlo Carerra; Carlo went with Tough Tony from Parkside. Fat Chubby went with Patty Catalano of the Columbos."

Frankie had been right about his friend Whack Whack: he was really feared at the top. Rastelli asked Brasco to kill him. That's when undercover agent Joe Pistone shed his identity as mobster "Donnie Brasco"; his bosses in the FBI pulled him out of the field and back to headquarters.

Four months later, in September 1981, a federal racketeering complaint was filed at the federal courthouse in Manhattan's Foley Square. It said, "On or about May 1981, the defendant Benjamin Ruggiero, also known as Lefty, and others known and unknown, murdered Alphonse Indelicato, Philip Giaccone and Dominic Trinchera by shooting them to death."

Ruggiero had told Brasco in the spring of 1980 that two capos loyal to the boss of the family [Rastelli] arranged to murder several fellow capos, including Alphonse Indelicato, Philip Giaccone, and Dominick Trinchera. This arrangement was made with the sanction of all of the organized crime bosses in New York, who Ruggiero referred to as the "Commission." Ruggiero admitted to Brasco that he and guys on Sonny Black's crew had committed the murders.

The arrest complaint, which also named Dominick "Sonny Black" Napolitano as a defendant, went on to say that the evidence was being put together by an undercover FBI agent. Using the name Donnie Brasco, the Fed had "successfully infiltrated one of the principal organized crime groups in the nation, known collectively as the Bonanno organized-crime family."

When Frankie read about all of this in the paper, it made sense. Donnie Brasco had been recruited into the Family by Lefty and both worked as part of Sonny Black's crew.

"We found out later that Brasco's real name was Joseph Pistone. He was a Special Agent with the FBI. Later on, Pistone writes this book about what he did. It became the movie *Donnie Brasco* with Al Pacino as Lefty and Johnny Depp as Brasco. In the movie, they show my uncle and the others guys being shot in the basement of a social club in Brooklyn. To this day, my family can't watch the film because the massacre scene is just too upsetting," says Frankie. "I am convinced Brasco was there when my uncle was murdered and did nothing about stopping it. Otherwise he wouldn't have had the details he had."

Which, of course, raises the following question: If government agent Joseph Pistone knew in advance that the massacre was going to take place, if he actually called Giaccone as Frankie maintains, why didn't the FBI try to stop it?

"I'll tell you why," says Frankie, "because it got some powerful guys out of the way without the government having to lift a finger to prosecute them."

It wouldn't have been the first time that members of the FBI looked the other way while felonies were being committed. As for Pistone, his information led to the indictment, trial, and conviction of senior members of the Bonanno Family on a variety of felony charges. Then things went from bad to worse.

The Bonannos had been greedy. Despite the message about Galante, they stayed in the drug business.

"The Bonannos were the mules bringing in heroin from Sicily," says Frankie. "Caesar Bonaventre was, like, the main player. He was using pizzerias all over the New York area to distribute the dope. Caesar and Baldo [Amato] were out in Roosevelt Field going to a pizzeria when somebody reported their blue Caddy circling the lot. The cops showed up, went through their car, and found a gun. That's what started the investigation."

It became known in the press as the "Pizza Connection" case and led to the further debasement and embarrassment of the Bonanno Family as all of their key players went away. There was a separate series of indictments and convictions of the remaining Bonanno Family hierarchy for heroin distribution. The other four crime families were so angry about the events, they punished the Bonannos, who were at their lowest strength.

"We [the Bonannos] didn't have a seat on the Commission for awhile," says Frankie.

His uncle was dead. Frankie had to think for himself now. He wasn't sure where to go or what to do. The only thing he knew for sure was that he wanted a new car.

He'd had the 1967 Rally Sports Corvette throughout his family's upheaval. It was time to move on to a new car. Maybe that would help get his mind off the dull ache he felt every time he thought of his Uncle Philly.

PART TWO: THE FREELANCER

Chapter Three

PONTIAC TRANS AM

The Warner Brothers crime films of the 1930s—particularly 1931's *Public Enemy* starring James Cagney in his career-making role and any film with Humphrey Bogart or Edward G. Robinson—succeeded in showing the kind of poverty and social conditioning that produced the original group of gangsters that ruled the rackets in the first part of the century to 1931. Reality intruded in 1932.

That year, on the boardwalk in Atlantic City, three men took a walk. What they discussed was a blueprint for organized crime in New York. If executed well, it would ensure that the operation would eventually control a network that would infiltrate all fifty states. The story may be apocryphal, but there is no denying the facts.

At some point in 1932–33, Charles "Charley Lucky" Luciano (a.k.a. Lucky Luciano), Benjamin "Bugsy" Siegel, and Meyer Lansky came up with the idea of organizing crime. The "Outfit" was Lucky Luciano's name for this brand of crime that the three men introduced into the U.S. The two tough Jews and their brilliant Italian counterpart came up with the rather civilized concept of killing only for monetary gain: monetary gain was everything. Eventually, Luciano's "Outfit" would become a nationwide group of well-organized criminals run by the Five Families of New York.

With Mob family ties that stretched back to his great-grandfather Joseph, Frankie's career path was as good as chosen. And while Philly Lucky was dead, his name still translated into respect. Frankie was a restless young man and wanted to start making a name for himself within the Outfit.

Using the juice that his uncle's reputation still carried, Frankie formed his own crew of young independents: Mikey Hollywood ("as handsome as a Ken doll") from the Genovese Family; Larry Zano and his brother Junior, also from the Genovese; and Chris Cappanelli, his brother Anthony, and Mikey Paradiso from the Gambino Family.

"Everyone was tied in and we all hung out and did stuff together," Frankie recalls. "We all had thousands in cash in our pockets from the sale of the [stolen] goods. We started hanging together. We did armed robberies of drug dealers—never civilians. See, Chris was selling pot, coke—stuff like that. We'd make ten to fifteen K on the sale of the drugs. But it wasn't enough. Why bother buying the shit when we could steal it? Instead of making ten or fifteen, we'd get thirty. We'd rob the dealer and unload the shit ourselves. We didn't care who we robbed, if they were connected or not. And that started it. That was our specialty. That became our full-time job: findin' guys who were buyin' from the dealers, getting their routines down and goin' in when they'd have the most cash or product.

"Our main guy for getting rid of the stuff was Tony Armente, who was a Bonanno soldier. Sometimes, when we didn't have anybody lined up to take off, we'd buy from Tony. You gotta understand; this guy would kill you, stab you in the heart (to stop you from bleeding), cut your throat, hang you upside down in the shower to drain your blood, cut you into ten different pieces, and carry them out in a bunch of American Tourister luggage. Tony would bury you out in this bird sanctuary on Staten Island also called 'Boot Hill.' Tony was on *America's Most Wanted*. Tony's now doing about four hundred years in jail."

Of all the wiseguys Frankie met in this period of his life, the one he formed a lasting friendship with was Michael "Mikey Hollywood" Groak. Mikey had an unusual background for a wiseguy. His father was a New York City detective, first-grade, who became the president of the Patrolman's Benevolent Association, the chief negotiating arm of the NYPD. Mikey had rebelled against his father's life as a lawman. Instead, Mikey chose the fast, dangerous, monied life of a gangster.

"Mikey was as tough as they come. We started scheming, robbing. We got into the cigarette, cigar, and liquor business. Sometimes we'd take a truck down to North Carolina where we'd scam wholesalers outta a hundred thousand dollars of cigarettes, then bring it back and sell 'em. Most times we'd place orders at cigarette wholesalers. We'd come up with some phony name for our restaurant or club or tell them we were opening up a bunch of newsstands, give them an address of an abandoned building, and then have them ship hundreds of cartons of cigarettes to it. We'd pay them with phony certified checks that we printed up ourselves on a regular check writer."

Through such scams, Frankie and Mikey started racking up the dough and Frankie's criminal career as an independent started to take off.

"Then Tommy D came over. He said he'd heard about how well I was doing, that I was a good earner. The bottom line with these guys is money. He wanted me with him 'cause I had a reputation as a mover. Fuck him—I couldn't stand the son-of-a-bitch!"

Frankie wanted to steer clear of the Bonannos, not just because they killed his uncle but because the politics of the Family were in such disarray. With Rastelli in power, the Family had lost face. The idea of associating with just one Family seemed to have its liabilities.

"I didn't want to end up like my uncle. He had been a Bonanno his whole life; he'd been loyal to them then they clipped him and buried him somewhere. I began to think about going a different way. I wanted to move around freely. I didn't want anybody bustin' my balls. I wanted to do business with any crew. Everyone stuck to their own crew. If I wasn't with any crew, I could move around and not answer to anyone."

Frankie never read any of the self-help books of the 1980s, but he followed some of their best advice: Make money doing something you love. Only he didn't quite do it in the way the self-help gurus had in mind.

"Basically, it really *was* a body shop. Continental Auto Body was the name of it. We started out actually doing collision work in Islip. I used to paint cars. I actually liked it; it was very relaxing. Did that for a while. My firm was doing very well. Then I started seeing there was a lot of money in parts, especially bumpers."

Bumpers?

"Do you remember at the time in the early eighties in New York when there were all these Caddies riding around without front bumpers?

It was the biggest thing to rob; people just wanted them—I don't know why. Who cared? I was getting a thousand dollars just for the bumper. Corvette t-tops [the glass roofs] were also huge at the time. You couldn't park your Corvette anyplace without having the t-top stolen."

Frankie had his own crew of car thieves roaming the night streets, shadows passing through the orange sodium streetlights. Frankie followed the old adage: waste not, want not. These were kids restless to make their way up in the Mob's chain of command. Frankie sold them on his scam as a way of making the bosses sit up and take notice. Working for Frankie was the path of career advancement. The bigger their earnings, the more the bosses noticed.

"The parts business brought in a lot of money but there was a lot of labor involved. It's easier to just sell the whole car. Trans Ams, Camaros, Corvettes—they were real big then. And also at the time, I had a guy. He was a good friend, name of Patty Testa. He was a made guy with the Gambinos. He actually had an auto body place in Flatbush on Utica Avenue.

"Patty was exporting stolen cars out of the country. Patty and his brother Joey were with Roy DeMeo, who ran a crew for Nino Gaggi, a skipper with the Gambinos. My Uncle Jimmy Clemenza was friends with Roy. That's how I met that whole crew. They were my friends since I was a kid. I did a ton of business with Roy, Patty, and Joey—all of them.

"The way it worked, Patty'd call me up and give me an order. 'I need two Lincoln Towne cars, Frankie. I need a black Coupe DeVille. I need a Buick Riviera,' Patty would say.

"We'd agree on the price, which was usually twenty-five hundred a car. I'd get my guys to go out and get 'em at night and the next day I'd go down to the Gemini Lounge where Patty worked. We'd park the cars on Utica Avenue, Avenue M—whatever—and leave 'em with the keys under the mat and he'd give me ten, twenty thousand—whatever it was."

The Gemini Lounge had a reputation.

"The Gemini Lounge. A fuckin' wild joint," says Frankie, laughing. "You didn't want to be in the Gemini Lounge at the wrong time when anybody was on drugs or fucked up. That crew killed a lot of guys: everyone knew they were nuts. I don't think they ever killed anybody for money. When Nino Gaggi needed work done, he went there. They fucked up a lot of guys. Roy was shooting to get his button; if you got in his way, you went.

"The Gemini, it was, like, a lot of knotty pine—that old beamed look. Bar on the right, tables on the left. When I'd walk in, I'd see Joey Testa sitting at one table. He was a fucking homicidal maniac. Sometimes I'd see Richie the Ice Man there. He was another one."

Richie did a lot of "contracts" for the Gambinos.

"There was a door that led to the back; there was an apartment back there. I never saw the Gorton Fishermen outfits [that protected the gangsters' clothes from victims' blood], but I heard the stories. But see, you don't ask questions. There are no daily gangster announcements: 'Who'd you clip this week?' These guys are friends of mine; I never looked at it in a frightening way. I was going to see Joey—we're all friends. And Roy? He was always a gentleman with me. I didn't worry about his temper or any of that shit. I was a kid—what did I know? I thought I was invincible. If it was today, I would still do business with them, but I'd have a fuckin' pistol on me, safety off."

Frankie's business dealings with DeMeo and his crew came to an abrupt end on January 10, 1983. Skipper Nino Gaggi allegedly clipped DeMeo, then stuffed the corpse in the trunk of DeMeo's own car. The killing had supposedly been carried out at the behest of Gambino boss Paul Castellano, who had grown tired of DeMeo's arrogance and indiscriminate killing, which was bad for business. Castellano had first asked his underboss John Gotti to do the job, but the future "Dapper Don" politely refused. Gotti would eventually kill Castellano and supplant him as boss.

"I fucking hated Gotti and so did everyone else. The son of a bitch brought more attention to wiseguys than anyone did. Every time [federal prosecutor and later NYC mayor] Giuliani prosecuted him, we kept rooting for his conviction."

But that was in the future. Frankie still had to make a living in the present. With DeMeo out of the way, he needed a new outlet for his car theft business.

"I started dealing with a guy on the Island—Bones. He had a Nissan dealership in front and a used body shop in the back." Whatever their suspicion, the legitimate workers at the dealership kept their mouths shut. You didn't have to be brilliant to figure out that if you opened your mouth to the cops, you'd wind up in Gravesend Bay. The water was so foul there, it actually dissolved metal; flesh was no problem.

"Now, I'm dealing with Bones and another guy who worked there— Sally Regina—overheard that I was the guy who got all the cars. He came up to me and started talking to me about cars and shit and I didn't trust him too much. I don't really want to deal with this guy. I really wouldn't talk to him. I just didn't trust him; there was something about him, like he's listening too close or something. But fucking greed takes over. I let Rico handle him. I wouldn't talk to him. But my partner Rico—man, did he talk."

At the time, Frankie's partner in the parts and stolen car business was Rico Marino.

"Rico starts dealing with Sally Regina. I'd go to Regina's house and I really wouldn't talk. But my partner Rico starts asking, 'What do you want? Tell me what you need. We can get you anything.' He put us in such a hole, that kid, with his mouth.

"One time we were over at Regina's house where we'd drop the cars off and we're in the garage. And Regina says, 'Oh, my phone's ringing,' and he runs back in the house. [I find out later] the batteries are fucking up on the wire he's wearing. I find that out later on when my lawyer gets the tapes. The only thing they have me on tape saying is, 'To be honest with you, I really don't want to deal with you, you look like a cop to me.' The guy, of course, denies it."

Six months went by. On a bright July day in 1984, Frankie and Rico went to Sally Regina's house to make a delivery.

"We go to his house with a brand new stretch Caddy with five hundred miles, a T-1 Porsche, and a 1984 Riviera. We're in the driveway and the money's about to change hands when all of a sudden this guy pulls up in a white Caddy wearing—I'll never forget—a black Members Only jacket. A gray-haired guy. Regina introduces him.

"'Oh, this is my partner Terry.' I said, 'Partner? What are you talking about?'"

Frankie was angry. And suspicious. Suddenly, after dealing with Regina for awhile, he suddenly has a partner that crawls out of the woodwork? Something just wasn't right.

"I walk away. Rico stays there and he's talking to the guy. I'm telling him, 'Are you out of your fucking mind? Look at that guy! That guy's a cop!' So after awhile, this guy Terry drives off. And I'm standing in the driveway and going to get my car to leave. And I see a squad car come down the street and I'm, like, 'What the fuck? Nah. You know, this can't be.' You know how you get that feeling? 'Nah, this can't be for real.'"

But it was.

"Sure enough the fucking police car pulls right into the fucking driveway. I go to turn and run and all I see are guys coming from everywhere. About ten cops run through a neighbor's yard, destroying his plants, and jump over the back fence and some hedges, and then they jump me—about ten of them—cuff me, and get me up. Unmarked cars pull up."

Usually, when a suspect is arrested in Suffolk County on Long Island, they are taken to the closest precinct for booking. But not Frankie and Rico.

"They take us directly to the District Attorney's Office in Hauppage and right up to the Rackets Bureau. They read us our rights and started questioning us—Rico too. They gotta make a production out of it so we don't think he set us up. They tell us how bad they got us, how they got us transporting stolen cars interstate, which is a federal beef."

The cops were making Frankie out to be the mastermind of a major car ring. Which he was. But at the time, Frankie didn't have the perspective to see that. He simply considered himself a guy on the way up, just trying to make a living any way he could. As far as he was concerned, he wasn't hurting anybody. Everything he stole, he figured, was insured; everything he stole was new. Who cared if the insurance companies had to pay up?

"The outcome was they took us and arraigned us. I had gotten arrested a few years before when I was still a juvenile for a burglary. I got probation. At the time, my record from my first case was sealed. My father had made sure it was, because I'd been a minor; I got the [mug] pictures back and everything.

"So now this looks like my first arrest, not second. I know my first arrest was a 'B Felony'—I've had a little experience. And the cops start talking and saying this shit about wanting to help me and I stop 'em cold.

"'Listen, I want a lawyer.' Soon as I said that, everything stopped."

Which is the way it's supposed to be. Once a suspect asserts their constitutional right to an attorney, by law the questioning has to cease. But in Suffolk County, as a state commission would discover, that wasn't always the case. Suffolk County detectives were infamous for beating confessions out of suspects, regardless of what rights were invoked. With Frankie, though, there would have been no point. Uncle Philly had ingrained the code of omerta on Frankie's soul: there was no way he would talk. The cops, though, continued to try.

"They'd still come into the interrogation room where they were holding me—you know, the kind of place with a battered desk and chairs, and walls painted puke green? They'd try and scare me into talking: 'Oh, you'll get thirty years.' Stuff like that. Fuck that. Finally, they take me for arraignment. We get outside and what do I see out front? Parked in front of the DA's office are the stretch Caddy, the T-l Porsche, and the 1984 Buick Riviera. They were fucking with us.

"'Hey Frankie—does that look familiar? What do you think of that limo?' one of the cops asked.

"'That's nice, is it yours?' I asked him."

They drove Frankie and Rico to the arraignment "out east," as Long Islanders like to say, into the furthest recesses of Suffolk County, to the drab State Supreme Court Building in Riverhead—the county seat.

"Listen to this. The judge is Michael Mannone, my father's first cousin. He knows my name; he knows who I am. I go for arraignment and all they get me on was fifty counts criminal possession of stolen property in the first degree. The fucking judge—I got no criminal record now—the judge who's my cousin sets bail at half a million dollars! So my father gets this lawyer, Hal Jordan, a wiseguy lawyer out of the Woolworth Building in Manhattan. He comes back to the bullpen.

"'Frankie,' he says to me, 'Frankie, what the fuck was in the trunk of these cars?! What did you have, bodies in the trunk?' I tell him the judge must have a hard-on for me. I can't figure it out.

"'Look Frankie,' he says, 'I got another bail hearing scheduled for next week, so you're gonna have to lay up a little bit.' I go the next week for the bail hearing before Judge Mannone and he reduces my bail to forty thousand cash and I get out."

Frankie was only out for two days before he went back down to the Nissan dealership to talk to the owner, Bones.

"I grab the guy and tell him, 'You got a fucking rat, bro. This guy's wearing a wire and everything.' The guy didn't want to hear it; the guy's blowing me off. 'You gotta be a fucking rat too, then. I come here to do you a fucking favor and you're blowing me off and telling me to be quiet?'

"Now I end up thinking that Bones was involved too. So what happens is, I see that the kid, Sally Regina—he's in the back working in the shop, that muthafucker. Sally wasn't a cop; he was just a guy who got pinched for something and was setting guys up to get out of trouble. I go in there, I got a fucking crowbar, and I beat the fuck out of him. I bashed his skull in."

A person can easily die from being beaten with a crowbar, but Frankie "didn't really give a fuck at the time. I get home. By the time I get there, my lawyer already called. They were charging me with first-degree assault and revoking bail. I go down to turn myself in. My lawyer tells me, 'We take this to trial; there's no way we're gonna win. They got too much on you.'"

So Frankie did what he's good at: he made a deal.

"It was a score, actually. In return for dropping most of the charges against me [including the assault charge], I plead guilty to three counts of criminal possession of stolen property in the first degree. I went up before my cousin, Judge Mannone for sentencing, and he gave me four years."

Every prisoner in the New York State Correctional System has to go through preliminary processing at the Downstate Correctional Facility in Fishkill, NY. The place is about one hundred miles north of Long Island.

"I wait in the Riverhead jail until October—about four months—before they took me to Downstate. After I sign in and everything, they assign me to Clinton State Prison. It's in an upstate town called

Dannemora; most cons just call the prison Dannemora. So for a nonviolent felony, first offense, they send me to a Max A joint with perverts and murderers. There were guys doing three hundred years there."

He had merited such unusual first-time treatment because the Rackets Squad—whose chief target consisted of mobsters—prosecuted him. In other words, did Frankie receive a more severe punishment because the cops and court perceived him as a "known associate of organized crime" rather than an independent? Likely. Which is ironic, considering he *was* an independent. From the time of his uncle's murder he had remained unaffiliated. So far it was working—he didn't have to kick upstairs.

"A month before, I'd had my twenty-first birthday on September 10. And it's my first time in prison—it didn't feel too good. A fucking twelve- or fourteen-hour bus ride up to Dannemora and stopping at all these jails to pick up guys along the way.

"What they do is they shackle your feet and they have this thing they put around your waist and they handcuff you without any chain so there's no play. Then they take the handcuffs and clip 'em to this little black metal box around your waist. You can't move; you have no fucking movement. So I ride for fourteen hours on a bus like that. Fucking torture, bro—torture. They give you a fucking sandwich, right? Try to get the fucking sandwich into your mouth."

Frankie had been on the bus since the early morning. Even inside the bus with its closed windows, he could tell that the air had gotten colder. When they reached Plattsburgh, which is a little south of the Canadian border, the driver took a hard left. The bus rumbled along a dark, two-lane road—Route 374—for ten miles through the small town of Cadyville, then climbed the Cadyville Hills. At the top of the hill, the driver looked out his windshield. There, built into the side of a mountain, was Clinton State Prison. With a crackle of gears, the bus descended into hell.

The first building on the right is currently called the Annex. Large coils of razor wire surround it. Not long ago, it was the State Hospital for the Criminal Insane; the town residents called it "The Bug House." Now it's used to house inmates. When the bus finally arrived inside the prison walls at about midnight, Frankie got out and looked around.

The moon was half full and he could make out a series of buildings of all shapes and sizes. At the top of the buildings, silhouetted against the dark night sky, was the unpleasant image of barbed wire, twisted into ugly coils.

"This way," said a guard, and marched the prisoners inside a low-lying building.

Frankie marched, but kept looking around. He saw armed guards patrolling the grounds. He noticed the towers, set up at intervals around the prison; he could see the bare outline of the guards inside of them. He figured they must be marksmen carrying rifles fitted with sniper scopes, in case inmates were stupid enough to attempt an escape. He later found out that he was right.

"They took me in, processed me—name, prints, pictures, shit like that. Then they took me up to the cell block. It was fucking huge: an old maximum security cell block with one-man cells. Looked like something from one of those old movies. I start walking down the catwalk and everyone starts screaming, 'New jack, new jack,' throwing shit. For a twenty-one-year-old, it was a pretty wild experience."

When Frankie got to his cell he stopped for a second and then the guard pushed him in. In the four-by-six-foot cell he saw a bunk and a sink attached to a toilet. The overhead light was just a bare bulb and was so dim, he couldn't see. Basically, it was useless, "fucking dead." Frankie turned and faced the catwalk and that's when he heard the sound for the first time.

"The cells were cranked closed. There was a chain that went through every cell, attached to a wheel at the end of the gallery. The guard turns a crank and you hear 'Crrrrrr,' and the bars start moving, then, 'Bang.'"

The bars hit home, sunk into the three-foot thick walls. Frankie looked around at his new home, out at the other cells, and listened as the screams died down until all that could be heard was snoring. He sat down on his bunk and suddenly, he began to think about his Uncle Philly, who had never been arrested in his life. Yet here he was in one of New York State's worst prisons for a nonviolent felony.

"I just didn't get it," says Frankie. "My uncle, he did so many things and never once got jailed. I really needed to figure it out."

Frankie would have time to do just that.

Chapter Four

SLOWED TO A CRAWL

From the J.H. French's *Gazetteer of the State of New York*, 1860:

> Pannemora was formed from Beekmantown, Dec. 14, 1854. It is the central town upon the west border of the county [of Clinton]. Its surface is mostly a wild, mountainous upland, covered with a sandy soil and light growth of forest trees. Chazy Lake, near the center, 3 1/2 miles long by 1 1/2 wide, discharges its waters east into Chazy River. Upper Chateaugay Lake, on the west border, 5 miles long by 1 1/2 broad, discharges its waters west into Chateauguay River. The few settlements in town are confined to the southeast corner. Dannemora is a small village grown up around the Clinton Prison. The prison was located here in 1845, for the purpose of employing convicts in the mining and manufacture of iron, so that their labor would not come so directly in competition with the other mechanical trades.

Clinton Prison is in the middle of the Adirondack Mountains, as far away from Frankie's New York as the dark side of the moon. In the Adirondacks, wild boar, deer, and even the occasional mountain lion, are more numerous than people. Towns are twenty or more miles apart. Civilization really is half a century away.

Clinton was the third prison the state built to rehabilitate convicts, the most notorious being Sing Sing Prison in Ossining, known as "The

Big House," followed by Auburn Prison in Auburn. When older gangsters like Frankie's uncles Philly Lucky and Jimmy Brown said that one of their kind had "Gone up the river," they meant he had been sent to jail at Sing Sing. Even further upstate, Clinton was just as bad and just as notorious for its cutthroat clientele that were housed in a prison built when Abraham Lincoln was a young man. By the time Frankie Saggio got there in 1985, Clinton was clearly outdated. Put another way, the place was nothing short of a hellhole.

Prison's not a good place to begin with—you're locked up behind bars, for one. You can't go anyplace for the length of your term. Clinton housed some really bad guys whose crimes had put them behind bars for a year or more.

In our society, first-time felony offenders, even those who have mugged people, frequently get probation with no jail time. By the time you are sentenced to a jail term, you've had to do enough damage for the state to be willing to spend its precious money to house you for awhile. It was men in this category who became Frankie's fellow inmates, the people he would see every hour of every day for the next eighteen months. That was the bit Frankie needed to do before they let him out—assuming, of course, he didn't do anything that would keep him in longer. Frankie had an advantage there.

He was a good enough businessman to know that prison was not a wise investment. He could immediately see there was no money to speak of to be made in jail. The only thing that counted was survival and filling your bit so they didn't tack anything on to it.

Every third guy was like Frankie: just some kid sowing his oats who'd done something nonviolent to make some quick money. And now those smart-aleck kids who thought they'd beaten the system had been thrown in with guys just waiting to devour such fresh meat and turn them into bitches.

"The way it works in jail, if you don't throw the first punch you become a maytag," says Frankie. "That means you're a bitch; you wash some guy's clothes, you do whatever he wants."

Which includes sex.

"Of course! Whatever he wants. If you don't fight in jail—especially that jail—that's what you are: a bitch. So I'm there one fucking day. A fucking day! I'm in the mess hall. And I get into a fight with a guy who said something to me I didn't like. So I take this guy on and I get a ticket. That means I have to answer for my actions in a kangaroo court of fucking guards. Plus, I automatically get an 'inciting a riot charge' added to my ticket. That comes from fighting in the mess hall where there's five hundred people who could actually bust some guards' heads at any moment.

"Then you gotta go before the sergeant for a hearing. You're going there to plead your case, which don't mean shit. It just means you're going in there to find out how long you're gonna be locked in. They gave me three months in the box. The box is basically a cell smaller than the one I was in. It doesn't have bars—it's got a steel door."

The box is true solitary confinement, designed by nineteenth-century minds for the purpose of severe punishment. It entails complete segregation: no contact with other individuals.

"A fucking rotty, disgusting, horrid shithole!" is how Frankie remembers it. "A steel door with a flap in it. All that's for is to slide a [food] tray in. The toilet don't work and the sink don't work. Fucking roaches everywhere. You'd wake up in the morning and you'd see three dead roaches under you that you rolled over on the night before.

"There's no light, no window. You don't know when it's day; it's always night. The only light comes from the cracks in the door. You tell the time by your meals: breakfast comes at six, lunch comes at eleven, and dinner comes at four. After that point, you got no fucking clue. No books, no magazines, no newspapers."

There are three kinds of guys in solitary. The first type just cracks. Schizophrenia among prisoners in solitary is not uncommon. The second type gets angry and decides to get back at the guards, whom the prisoner blames for their incarceration. What they do is take their human waste, ferment it until it stinks to high heaven, and then throw it into the faces of the guards at the first opportunity.

Frankie describes the consequences of this course of action. "If you have a brain, you don't play with the guards. Throw something at those guys and the goon squad comes in: eight guards crammed into a six-by-eight-foot cell beat you down."

The third type of guy in solitary is like Frankie. He knows the score and does his best to get through it.

"I'll tell you how I kept my sanity. I had a button from a cop's shirt that I ripped off on the way in. I played with that for three months. I counted the tiles on the floor, multiplied them, divided them, counted every screw and bolt I could see. I did push-ups till I dropped. That was the only way I could make myself tired."

To tell what day it was and how much longer he had in solitary, Frankie marked the wall. "I'd start putting marks on the wall. Then I decided to speed up the time a little and mark off the whole rest of the week. That ended up being too frustrating so I stopped doing it."

State law dictates that prisoners must be given one hour of exercise per day. Frankie outlines the Clinton Prison interpretation of that law: "They took me out handcuffed and shackled. I was the only person in the yard. They made sure no one was around. They put me in a cage in the yard where I couldn't sit down because it's only big enough to stand up in. And I'd just stand there till they took me back inside."

Frankie followed this boring routine for three months until they let him out and he went back into his cell and the general prison population.

"There was fighting all the time. Half the time you know you're gonna take a beating or give a beating, one way or another. As long as you fight—win, lose, or draw—you ain't a bitch. I got a vicious beating one time. I had a fight with a Puerto Rican kid." Frankie had only been out of solitary for a few days before he got in trouble again.

"We were boxing. I was a young guy, so I could fight. I got him a few times and then he got ahold of me. The last thing you want to do in a fight is let the other guy get ahold of you. This kid got on top of me and he punched my lights out. He left me there, all bloody and fucked up. I'd lost the fight. I was unconscious for what seemed like a second or two. When I come to, I see the kid walking away. To him, the fight's over. I remembered what my Uncle Philly used to say about picking up the nearest thing and bashing someone's skull in if they were messin' with you.

"So I looked around. There's a guy mopping the galley. The mop has a heavy steel ringer on it."

Before he could reach for the mop, Frankie saw the guards running toward him down the corridor. Who won the fight was irrelevant now; he and the Puerto Rican kid were going back to solitary for at least a six-month bit for fighting.

Frankie lurched to his feet. The kid started to turn.

"I grabbed the fucking mop and fucked him up. I fucking bashed him in the head so many times, he got fifty, sixty stitches in the head, a broke nose, and I knocked his teeth out. After that, I never had a problem again in that jail."

Frankie also didn't have a problem readjusting to the general prison population—he got another six in the box. To Frankie, beating the kid was worth it. He didn't care that during his first three weeks in solitary the second time he sat recovering from the bruising and battering he'd received in the fight. In the darkness of the cell, clutching the guard's button, waiting to be fed like an animal on a schedule, counting the cracks in the floor and the rivets on the door, doing endless push-ups to tire himself out, standing outside all alone in the cage in the yard, it was worth it. Nobody was going to get the better of him. It was that simple.

In the spring of 1985, Frankie was released from the box. Coming out of solitary, he had to shield his eyes against the dim overhead fluorescents that had replaced the previous century's gas lamps. Level by level, Frankie was led up through the bowels of the building by the guard's firm grip on his arm. Frankie began to hear the sounds of men shouting, laughing, screaming. He emerged into bright sunlight and closed his eyes, needing time to adjust to daylight again.

The guard led him across the yard. It was the first time Frankie had seen it filled with people. He saw large groups of men, seemingly segregated by appearance, milling about in their own sections. There was no overflow from one section to the other. Frankie instantly sized up what was happening: had there been overflow, there would have been a riot.

Back in his cell, Frankie looked around. His bunk looked like a fancy Sterns and Foster mattress compared with the flea-bitten, cockroach-infested thing he had slept on in solitary. The sink and toilet combination looked positively luxurious.

He'd been in solitary since his second day in Clinton. Now that he had established himself in the prison as a guy who took shit from nobody, he needed a little more juice to get through the rest of his sentence. He wasn't into fighting to prove his manhood—he fought to survive.

But there was an easier way. It was time to affiliate.

"In Clinton, there's all different courts in the yard. Guys have got their weights there. They got their tables to eat on. And they're all very segregated. There's the black court, with all the black guys; the Puerto Rican court with all the Puerto Ricans; the Italian court, where all the Italians stay. The Muslim court in another place, as is the court for the white supremacists, and the five percenters. The five percenters are the five percent of the elite population of the world who think they're better than everyone else is." Frankie knew the protocol from days of observing.

"You never just walk up and walk onto a guy's court. What you gotta do is walk around the yard. For weeks, maybe for a month. You don't talk to nobody, you don't do nothing, you just walk until somebody from a court comes over and says, 'Hey, come over to our court.' That's how it works. I didn't have to walk long. A guy came up to me and says 'We know you're Philly Lucky's nephew. Come over to our court.'"

The Italian Court at Clinton did not contain—as many in the prison population thought—all guys from the Outfit. The Outfit guys were actually in the minority. The rest were just hard-working crooks, schemers, perverts, and murderers like the rest of the prison population. But within the Italian court, it was the Mob guys who had the muscle and were not afraid to use it to keep themselves safe.

"There were three Columbo guys there: Johnny Fish; Pete Rugota, a guy from Kennedy Airport; and Ralphie Lombardi. Ralphie was doing twelve years at the time."

Lombardi would go on to become the consigliere of the Columbo Family.

"It was great to see those guys. They gave me hugs. It was just amazing, it really felt like home."

At home, Frankie had seen those guys all the time, whenever he wanted. In prison, they really didn't have time to get reacquainted.

"I did half my bit in the box—twelve months. A full year in [solitary confinement]. I did another three months at Dannemora in the yards.

Then one day in my fifteenth month the guard comes to my cell and says, 'Saggio, you're being transferred down the road.' They ended up shipping me to a camp called Lion Mountain that was fourteen miles down the road from Clinton. A minimum security prison. The criminals were low-level types, petty thieves mostly. No cell; I was in a dorm there with eighteen to twenty other guys."

Besides housing petty criminals, Lion Mountain essentially functioned as a halfway house for the Clinton cons up for parole. In Frankie's case, he reached his first parole hearing at the eighteen-month mark of his four-year sentence. If he got it, which was by no means assured, he would be released and be back on the street.

Parole hearings at Clinton took place in what Frankie remembers as a "dingy shithole, just like the rest of the place. It was a narrow, cramped, smelly room. Puke green walls. It was just me and three parole guys."

On one side of a battered table sat Frankie, ready to plead his case for parole. On the other side, sitting with stony faces, were three people from the parole commission. Spread out in front of them on the faded faux wood finish of the conference table was Frankie's file, thick with legal documents. Near the top were copies of the two fighting tickets, the first of which included the "inciting a riot" charge.

"The parole commission, they understand and they know that your record inside is never good. They understand and they know that fighting's part of jail and that's what happens. But it doesn't mean they ignore it. Fighting also shows you're not reforming yourself. I told them that I feared for my life and I reacted the way I thought I had to to save it."

Frankie didn't think that would be good enough.

"I figured they'd hit me with an extra year. Now, believe it or not, through all of this I got my high school diploma. I had four guys without teeth who were my fellow students. My teacher gave me his pen because I graduated at the top of my class," he says, laughing. "I guess that was because I had all my teeth."

Getting his diploma could help Frankie's case. It showed some sort of rehabilitation on his part, but he couldn't be sure.

"Look," he says matter-of-factly, "you're either going home or you're not going home. And when the hearing's over, they don't tell you which.

They notify you by mail. Like I said, I thought they'd hit me with another year but I got the letter about a week later telling me that I got parole. At that point, I still got two more months to do to reach the eighteen months, which is when I get my parole. Because I'm in the minimum security camp and because I made parole, they [rewarded] me with a furlough to go home for five days."

Frankie got back onto a bus to go down to the Island, but this time he wasn't chained, he wasn't manacled, and he wasn't guarded. He was a free man for five days.

Frankie looked around his parent's home in Deer Park and couldn't believe he was there. Nothing had changed in the sixteen months he'd been inside. It was the same furniture, the same carpeting, the same bed, the same parents. His mother Petrina cooked him all his favorites. For the five days he was there he gorged on peppers and eggs, fresh homemade lasagna and ziti, and fried calamari in diavolo sauce. There were creamy cannoli and Frankie's favorite: a sesame seed, poppy seed, onion, and salt bagel—called an "everything" bagel—toasted to perfection with a generous "shmear" of cream cheese.

"Perfect clogging-the-arteries food," Frankie laughs.

At the end of the five days, Frankie took the Long Island Railroad into Pennsylvania Station at 34th Street in Manhattan. Through tiled corridors that smelled of urine and stale sweat, he made his way to the Amtrak platforms in the back of the station. The prison system had given him a bus ticket, but he was sick and tired of buses. He gave the ticket away to some homeless guy who gave him the kind of look that said, 'What the hell am I supposed to do with this?' and went into his own pocket for train fare.

Frankie gazed out the window as the train started up. Soon it came out of the tunnel on the other side of the Hudson River and proceeded up the lower Hudson Valley. Explorer Giovanni da Verrazano had not ventured this far north back in 1524 when he became the first European to enter New York Bay and discovered Long Island. The discovery of the river that led north through the mountains was left to Captain Henry Hudson, the Dutch explorer who charted it during a trip in 1609. Hudson, who named the river after himself, went as far north as Albany; Frankie had to go much further.

The Amtrak right-of-way was next to the river and the trip provided spectacular views of the Hudson River estates owned by families named Vanderbilt and Roosevelt, among many others. About ten hours after the trip began, Frankie made Plattsburgh. Then he hopped a local bus that traveled through the mountains on its way to the minimum security prison.

"So I was back in the Lion's Mountain camp. I kept my nose clean; I had nothing left to prove. And I really had nothing to do for those last two months. Except think. I knew I didn't want to go away again. I kept thinking how my Uncle Philly never went away once; he wasn't even charged. It amazes me to this day."

Frankie remembered how his uncle had more than one legitimate business to shield the money made from his other, illegal ones. Frankie was determined to do the same. He was also determined to settle down. It had worked for his uncle, why not for him? He was still stuck on his former next-door neighbor, Anna Gambino. He wrote to her. She wrote back that she really wanted to see him again.

"Anna was an old-fashioned Sicilian girl. She was born there. All she wanted was a husband, a house, and a kid."

On June 7, 1986, Frankie Saggio stepped out into freedom. "It was unbelievable. They let me go right there at Clinton. They gave me forty dollars and a blue polyester suit and a bus ticket back to the Port Authority. First thing I did was go into a bathroom and change. My mother had sent me a sweat suit, shirt, and sneakers. No way I was wearing that blue poly suit. I threw it right in the garbage."

At the bus terminal, Frankie found the bus with the sign "New York" over the passenger cab and got on.

"It was the best bus ride I ever took in my life. Anna picked me up at the Port Authority and drove me home."

Between his business and professional life, Frankie figured he had a good future ahead of him. But no one lives in a vacuum, least of all a gangster who was part of the Five Families.

Chapter Five

LINCOLN TOWNE CAR, COUPE DEVILLE, CHEVY CORVETTE

Not everyone who's Italian and has a Mob name is a wiseguy. Take Ricky Gambino.

Ricky was a cousin to Carlo Gambino, the boss of the Gambino Family. He was as clean as the proverbial whistle. Ricky had established the largest marble and granite supply business in the United States without the assistance of the Outfit. He also happened to be a good friend of Philip Giaccone.

"Ricky lived next door to my uncle. My uncle loved Ricky," says Frankie.

Philly Lucky appreciated the effort of a hard-working immigrant like Ricky, who had established his business honestly. Philly Lucky wasn't about to corrupt that effort.

"Ricky had two daughters, Anna and Sandra. I was stuck on Anna. I was Anna's first boyfriend. She came from a good family. My family was close with hers. It seemed like a natural."

Anna was what Mob guys call a civilian, and Frankie was going to marry her. Anna was a Sicilian beauty. She was of medium height and had dark skin and a knockout, voluptuous figure. She knew what Frankie was and didn't care; or if she did, she never showed it. To Frankie, her tastes were simple; she would be content to marry, have children, and be what was called a "homemaker" in America in the late 1980s.

In 1987, at the age of twenty-three, Frankie married Anna Gambino. It was as practical a deal as any he had ever made.

"I had not one, but two weddings: one in Italy and one in America."

Frankie's American wedding was as well attended as any Mob wedding. Frankie had a blast. Mikey Hollywood was his best man. Afterward, Frankie bought a house in Dix Hills near his Aunt Annette, Philly Lucky's widow, though it wasn't quite as extravagant. To act as a cover for what he was really doing, he opened a legitimate trucking business, Big Apple Trucking and financed its operation from his illegitimate activities.

"At that point, we were doing a lot of stickups, me and Mikey Hollywood—all drug dealers. They were great targets. They ain't callin' no cops and ain't runnin' to no wiseguys and even if they were kickin' up to a goodfella, it would never be admitted 'cause Mob rules are that dealin' drugs is punishable by death. I was actually doing very well. I was probably doing about—take home—about a hundred seventy-five thousand a year. You know, somewhere around there. But see, part of the fun in making the money was *how* we did it.

"One time we're on a job and Mikey's got a fucking .22 Ruger with a silencer—the choice of button men. It's the only pistol you can really silence. Anyway, Mikey's clip keeps falling out of the gun. I was cracking up. Mikey gets so frustrated he turns to me and says, 'Take this fucking gun, gimme yours!' Mikey would always make me laugh. But the sick bastard couldn't make an auto work."

In 1990, Frankie's father, Dennis Saggio, died from a congenital heart condition. Because of his hemophilia, he had been in and out of hospitals for years. Uncle Philly had taken on the role of father during Frankie's earlier years but after Philly was killed, Frankie got to know his own father better. Frankie had gotten to the point in life where he was an equal with his father. Illness took that pleasure away.

Frankie was broken up by his grief. First his uncle, then his father—the two most important men in his life, dead. But he had little time to recover. He had to survive. To survive in the Mob, he needed to keep making money.

Frankie had now been a gangster since his teens and had spent almost a decade as an earner. He was probably the only member of the Mob to actually look at his illegal businesses as a profession. Within his world of the Five Families, Frankie was getting a reputation as an intelligent mover and shaker, and a kid with balls. The bosses had their eye on him.

They would make more money off of him and his deals than off all the bullshit shakedown artists that manned the Families' crews put together.

"I always tried to hide the money I made from the bosses. I knew the way the tax worked: ten percent off the top of everything gets kicked upstairs in the envelopes, like the one I pulled out of my Uncle Philly's pocket when I was a kid. So I never told the skippers an accurate figure. If I made eighty, I told them I made twenty. I was always kicking upstairs to the bosses, but never what I really should have."

Frankie really thought he could get the better of the guys who knew every trick in the book they themselves had written.

One those guys was having his own troubles, and Frankie couldn't have been happier.

Rusty Rastelli may have been Machiavellian when it came to assassinating rivals and maintaining power, but he was totally inept when it came to dealing with the Feds. He couldn't stay out of trouble. As soon as he was released from jail in the late 1980s, the Feds mounted another case against him and won.

Sixty-eight-year-old Rastelli and his head capo, Joey Massino, were convicted of bribery and extortion involving Teamsters Local 814, moving and storage workers. The judge sentenced Rusty to twelve years in prison. But Rusty was getting old. This time, he wouldn't be able to rule the Family as he had during his last stay away. Once again, there was a power vacuum in the Bonanno Family. Essentially, the Family was rudderless.

Frankie had broken away from the Bonannos five years earlier to run his own crew of independents when his uncle had been killed, but he had not affiliated elsewhere. Prison had taught him the value of affiliation. So now it was Frankie's turn to be a fence-jumper. But which Family?

Colombo? Gambino? Genovese? Lucchese? Frankie knew guys in all of them. His Uncle Jimmy, who was still alive, had been a capo in the Profaci/Columbo Family before he retired to North Carolina where he was a mainstay at Duke University's Rice Diet Clinic. Uncle Jimmy was a top Mob assassin who liked to lose weight using the trendiest of diets.

But back to the problem. Who to affiliate with?

"I had had a bar at around the same time. It was on Long Island, next to the OTB [off-track betting) in Sayville. The name of the place was Ringside Sports Club; it was a sports bar. And in the back, me and a guy called Joey Black—who was another guy with Tough Tony from Parkside—were running a blackjack and craps game out of the kitchen. So what happens is, me and Joey are doing really good; we're doing, like, four or five thousand a weekend running the game on a Friday and Saturday. Now to get the players, I got a guy that's in OTB—this guy, Vern—and he's pulling players for me because I was right next door to the OTB. So I would send him in the OTB all day and he would pull guys for me. Guys making bets, he would make friends with guys, you know, 'I got a crap game, I got a blackjack game, I'll take you guys to it—' blah, blah, blah. And he'd bring 'em back.

"And there was a guy who used to hang out in the OTB, his name was George the Shylock. So Vern, who was an imbecile, comes up to me and says, 'Frankie, there is a shylock that hangs out in the OTB. I want to introduce you to the guy.' I said, 'Alright.' So he introduced me to the guy and the guy comes off like a gangster and all this shit. I know the guy is a jerk-off, you know what I mean?"

What Frankie means is that any guy who tries to act like a gangster, really isn't one. He doesn't have the utter ruthlessness that comes with a generations long pedigree.

"So I tell the guy, 'Alright, you know what? I need twenty grand.' He gives me the big rundown of how good he is at collecting money and this and that. And he gives me the twenty for points.

"In other words, he thinks he's loaning me the money. He doesn't think he's just giving me the money, he thinks I'm borrowing it. So I think, at the time, he wanted five hundred a week. Yeah, I think it was two-and-a-half points vig. Me and Joey got the card game going—we got about four or five players. George comes in the bar; he gives me the twenty thousand.

"'OK George, I'll see you next week,' I said. Anyway, he comes to me the following week. I tell him I don't have the money, to check with me the following week. I just gave him the runaround. I never gave him a nickel back. So he got loud with me one day in the bar. He starts acting

like a gangster. He says, 'You know, I'm with a
means you're under his protection.

"'Listen, go wherever you gotta go,' I told him.

"'I'm with Tony from Parkside,' he said.

"'Well, when you go to Tony from Parkside, you tell
Carerra's nephew and I took the money off you.' I really w
nephew, but I might just as well have been because I knew him
life."

A week later, Carlo Carerra called Frankie at his bar. Carlo had
on his Uncle Philly's Bonanno crew and fence-jumped to Tough To
Genovese crew after Philly Lucky's death.

"'You need to come down to the club in Parkside,' Carlo says. So I go
down there, to the Parkside Restaurant on 108th Street. The Parkside is
really a cafe that Tony owns. You know in Paul Simon's song 'Me and
Julio Down by the Schoolyard' there's a line about the Ice King of
Corona? That's a real store, right next door to the club. Anyway, Carlo
Carerra was already there and he took me to a table in the back where
we sat down and had some espresso. Then he starts.

"'Yeah, this guy George came in here crying this and that, he says you
took twenty large off him—badda beep, badda boop—and all this happy
horseshit. You haven't given him no money,' Carlo said, laughing.

"'Yeah, I took it off him,' I answered. So now we're, like, six months
into it and the guy is telling me that I owe him the thirty Gs plus twenty;
this guy wanted, like, fifty grand.

"'Alright, listen: Rom is going to come in.' Rom was Tony's street guy.
He used to run all the street business for Tony: the numbers, the
horses—everything. I've known Rom since I was a kid. I haven't seen
him in years, but he remembers me through my Uncle Philly, you know?
And now this is years and years later.

"'Frankie, listen,' Rom says. 'Throw me twenty-five, forget the vig.
I'll tell the guy when you got it you'll give it to him and not to come
around, not to bother nobody; you're over here, you're here, you're with
Tony.'"

"And that's how I ended up with Tough Tony from Parkside.
Remember, when you're with a guy, it means you are under his wing,

ke fucking with what we used
mess with anybody from

on't use his nickname to
ike my uncle was. He

mobster, Anthony
cord. He'd been
ts. But the only convic-
nses. Yet he was one of the most
ruthlessness in enforcing his edicts.
ne Parkside, you wouldn't even know he owns
walks around in a black Members Only jacket, black
eat pants, and a pair of high-top sneakers. And he doesn't talk
anybody, period, unless he knows you. If he knows you, he'll talk to
you. If he don't know you, he'll walk right past you. No matter what you
say, wave hello, ba, ba,—whatever—he's walking right past you.

"Across the street from the Parkside is Spaghetti Park. The neighborhood is mostly Hispanic now, but only Italians go in Spaghetti Park because Tough Tony *owns* that park. No one else. I mean, Tony maintains the Park, Tony paints the Park, Tony barbecues in the Park—it's Tony's park. He's got guys cleaning constantly: sweeping the park, cleaning this, doing that. Tony is, like, a fanatic with the Park, the restaurant, everything in that area. He's got guys sweeping the street over there.

"I can't tell you how many times I sat in the park with Tony. He loves White Castle. We would go to White Castle and then we would go sit in the park, watch the old men play bocci, eat the square burgers: me, him, and Mikey Hollywood. He loved Mikey because Mikey was a quiet, tough kid. And I brought him around and Tony just took an automatic liking to him. So there we are: me, Tony, Mikey, and a bag of White Castles. Just sitting in the park and talking. Tony was in his forties then and he'd been in the Mob a long time.

"'Frankie, this whole life is bullshit,' he told me. 'All this wiseguy stuff, it's all crap. A lot of guys are into drugs; nobody keeps their word.

Nobody cares about nothing, least of all honor. Just a lot of bullshit, a lot of gossip, and a lot of nonsense. Things aren't the way they used to be like when your Uncle, God rest his soul, was alive.'"

Tony remembered how the assassination of the three capos in 1981 still resonated seven years later in the Outfit. In all the Families, it was regarded as a watershed moment when the old values were jettisoned in favor of a more cutthroat sensibility, even among cutthroats. Now, honor and grace were considered business liabilities, and possessing them made gangsters worthy of being clipped.

In the decade stretching from "Philly Lucky's" death in 1981, Tommy D had gone from being a soldier kicked out of a crew to a full-fledged capo in the Bonanno Family. For the most part, he was a man to be respected. But Frankie still suspected that his rise within the Family was directly due to his involvement in his uncle's death. Philip Giaccone Jr. didn't have any of those concerns.

After his father's death, Philly Lucky's son had wisely affiliated with the Genovese Family, where he was an up-and-coming soldier. Philip Jr. began to romance Frankie's sister-in-law Sandra. By early 1991, they were engaged. Later that year, they got married at the Marina Del Rey, an extravagant catering hall in the Bronx. Among the wedding guests was Tommy D. Frankie recalls their encounter.

"'Tommy, hey, how are you?' I said to him.

"'I know that shylock George you fuckin' robbed. He's a friend a mine. You know what you did to the guy wasn't right. It fuckin' wasn't right,' Tommy answered.

"'Hey,' I answered him back, 'I didn't make the decision. The decision was made over at Parkside.' I went to turn and walk away from him and he fuckin' grabs my arm.

"'Tommy, get your fucking hands off me you fucking cock-sucker,' I told him.

"'I'm a fucking made guy—don't fucking talk to me that way,' Tommy screams back."

From across the room Petrina Saggio watched as her only son spat in the face of Bonanno capo Thomas "Tommy D" DiFiore. Before Tommy could react, Frankie's cousin Philip and Mikey Hollywood broke the scuffle up. Disgusted, Frankie walked away.

"Philip told me after that Tommy said, 'I should have threw him in the fuckin' bay. I'll kill that muthafucker.'"

Petrina gave Frankie a warning afterward. "Uncle Philly threw him out. This guy is going to have it in for you now. *Never* trust him."

Frankie was impulsive, not stupid. If he was going to maintain his independence in dealing with cutthroats like Tommy D, he knew it was time to become a big earner.

"At the time, I was involved with a brokerage firm on 50th and 3rd in Manhattan. And I was dealing with a couple of these Greek guys and two Russian guys. And they were coming up with these phony money orders. But they were shit. They were garbage. And I had some very good friends at the time—which I wouldn't name—who were legitimate guys in the printing business. And I had one I used to hang out with practically every day, you know? I'd eat lunch with him and we'd hang out and stuff. One day, I got him drunk and I actually made him print some money on the press, just kidding around. And it was amazing! This guy burned a [printing] plate and actually just ran off twenty money orders. And they were actually pretty good. Then he burnt the plate and burnt the money. You know, he was just drunk and he was just playing games.

"Maybe a month later I approached him with this idea of these money orders. The deal I'd set up, we were supposed to get two million for the whole deal. We print twenty-two million in money orders, I bring it to a broker, and he gives me what, ten percent or $2.2 million. My cost is the printing."

Frankie went back to his legitimate printer buddy.

"I told him I was going to give him two hundred thousand just to print them, just to do the job."

His friend accepted.

"All I had to do was bring him a sample of a real Traveler's Express money order. And man, did he do his job! They were amazing! OK, now we start shopping them around. We had a few different guys, that we were dealing with, that were going to move them or we were going to go with the best deal. When we started out, we wanted twenty percent and we ended up hooking up with another Genovese made guy who g[...] deal for ten percent on the whole load. In other words, we were[...] looking to sell them one, two, or five at a time; we wanted to sell them *all at once*. We had, like, ten cases of them and we wanted to do one deal—one shot, one time—and that was it. So what happens?

"We were dealing with a guy named Max Longo, who was also a Genovese soldier at the time. It was me and my cousin Philip; we're both Genovese at the time. Max had a bodyguard who used to drive him around—his name was Tony. Tony is, like, an ex-body builder, Mr. New Jersey Universe contender and all this shit. We had gone out a few times with this guy and Max Longo. And Max, through his driver and body-guard Tony, has a hook. The hook could have been anybody—an FBI agent, it could have been just a guy who moves a lot of swag, or a guy who was a bookmaker, a shylock, or anybody in that line of work.

"'Philip,' I told my cousin, 'every time we're talking, this guy Tony is always making like he's looking at something else, but you can tell he's listening to our conversation. He's always nervous. I don't like this sneaky cocksucker. I don't want to talk to this guy. I don't trust him.'

"'Oh, don't be ridiculous—he's with Max,' Philip tells me.

"'I won't deal with him,' I told my cousin. I don't want nothing to do with the guy.'"

Frankie walked away from a deal that would have netted him $1 million in cash because he wouldn't take the chance of going back to prison. He knew that his uncle would have done the same: gone with his instincts instead of greed. But not Philly Lucky's son.

"My cousin Philip ends up continuing the deal on his own. This guy Tony," Frankie continues with derision, "tells my cousin Philip he needs a sample. 'I've got a guy who wants to take them; he needs a sample of what we got,' he says. So my cousin goes and gives him a stack of maybe a hundred phony money orders. If he would have got caught with just one, he probably wouldn't have got time. But he gave the guy a stack."

Frankie wasn't there when the money orders changed hands. His instincts had led him to do something else that day.

"Matter-of-fact, my sister called me. I was in Howard Beach on the way home when my sister Lina phoned me. 'They just broke into

'They grabbed him,' she added, 'they' meaning

house?' I asked.

had the rest of the money orders in boxes in his

got the whole load, they would up the charges. I called my sister-in-law, Philip's wife, and she said nobody searched the house yet. I told her, 'Light the fireplace, I'm on my way.' So I shot to my cousin Philip's house, got in, and threw ten cases of money orders into his fireplace and burned them. It took a couple of hours."

The Feds got a warrant a day later and searched Philip Giaccone Jr.'s house. They found nothing. Frankie had seen to that.

"My cousin, because he had no criminal record or anything like that, he ended up getting five years. He did a year and change and came out. He is still on federal parole."

As for the guy who had the hook, Max Longo got five years in jail. After that deal went south, Frankie sat in Spaghetti Park with Tough Tony. The two of them were alone, save for their square hamburgers and two little Italian men playing bocci. Tony listened and smiled when Frankie told him what had happened. Suddenly, Tough Tony's demeanor changed when he spotted two hawks overhead, circling the pigeon coop on top of his restaurant across the street.

Despite his curmudgeonly appearance, Tony was an old softy when it came to his pigeons. He had a group of prize racing pigeons that he kept on the roof of the Parkside Restaurant. He really loved them. And when those hawks starting circling, they were menacing his babies.

Tony raced across the street, went into the restaurant, and grabbed a 20-gauge Remington shotgun. Mounting the ladder to the roof, he took a position on one knee like an infantryman and fired at the hawks. He missed. But cops in a squad car passing the Parkside Restaurant heard the shots, came running, and arrested Tony on menacing and weapons charges.

"That's Tony," says Frankie, "Crazy and mellow at the same time. He'd seen that everybody in this life of ours was full of shit. There was a younger bunch of guys coming in at the time and things were changing. They carried briefcases for crissakes, like they were some fucking yuppies. There was so much money being invested by the bosses in legitimate businesses, from stocks to entertainment.

"Tony could stay on the roof. I needed to get in on that action."

Chapter Six

COUPE DEVILLE

It was in the shadow of the last days of the first Bush Administration in 1992 that the Mob began its assault on Wall Street. There was more money to be made there than anyplace else. The trick was to get a hook into a firm, bring the wiseguys in, and then exploit the situation.

Frankie remembers how he got in on the action. "Anna's cousin Marty was training to be a stockbroker. He gets hooked up with this guy who opens up a firm in Manhattan—Robert Todd Securities. The firm starts out legit. Marty starts having problems with some guys who are trying to butch in on the action and he calls me up.

"'Listen Frankie, we're having a few problems with some guys. Could you stop down? I want to talk to you.'

"I go down there and he's got a guy from the Columbos, Vint Bonner, trying to shake him down. Bonner had gotten in because he had a friend who was a broker there. And Bonner, he starts lending out money to a few brokers in the same firm. Once a shylock is floating you money, then he's got you. And those brokers? Those brokers were all just a bunch of sick, fucking, diseased, degenerate gamblers. They spent it as soon as they made it. They never kept any of it.

"So I go in and I meet Marty and I tell him, 'Look, your firm is with us [the Genovese Family].' Then we sit down and straighten everything out with the Columbos."

Once the Columbo guy realized the firm was with the Genovese, he left. Most mobsters would have ended it there. Instead, Frankie negotiated a straight percentage off the top of the brokerage's billings for his family without lifting a finger. Plus, he saw a real opportunity.

"'Marty, get me into this place. I want to do something here,' I tell him.

"This kid Marty is making twenty to thirty grand a month; a kid who used to work in a pizzeria for fucking ten years is making all this money. He's a good bullshitter and a good talker—he can sell guys anything. At that point, guys were taking tanning salons public. My idea was to get a license and my own crew in there and start selling securities."

Marty got Frankie into Robert Todd Securities.

"But I was a convicted felon so I couldn't get a license. What I had to do was use my brother-in-law's name to get my broker's license. I send my brother-in-law Kelly Scott to get a fingerprint card done in Georgia, at a local police station near where he lives. He gets the prints done and sends me back all the stuff. I give this to a Russian kid who we had go out and get an in-state driver's license in Kelly's name and use that as ID to take the stockbroker's test. This Russian kid was extremely intelligent. He'd charge me twenty-five hundred; otherwise, he's talking like anyone else. Then I made him take the manager's test and he charged me another thousand for that.

"Now I got a series twenty-seven and twenty-four manager's brokerage license and I'm in the firm. They blue sky me into all fifty states; in other words, I am licensed to sell stock anywhere: Texas, Utah—it didn't matter."

Frankie literally had what every crook covets: a true, unblemished, pristine, shiny license to steal.

"But I don't want to sit there and talk on the telephone. What I do is, I tell the vice president of Robert Todd, 'Listen, I'm going to hire twenty guys in here to cold call.' I start hiring a bunch of neighborhood kids— all street kids, all bullshit artists. Hustlers. Half of them didn't even have high school diplomas. And we're teaching them the business."

The men Frankie hired were what authorities like to call "Mob associates" from all of the Five Families. They were "Gen X'ers" Mob style, restless scammers who saw an opportunity to get across the Brooklyn Bridge and into Manhattan money by getting in on Frankie's scam.

Frankie was officially associated with the Genovese Family, and the bosses quickly became aware of the scam he was putting together. They had been waiting for the opportunity to make money off Philly Lucky's nephew and the moment had arrived. Not since the days of Bugsy Siegel, when the Mob united to make money off of legalized gambling in Las Vegas, had representatives from all Five Families united in a criminal conspiracy of such magnitude. And they had picked the best time to do it.

Many people have questioned Bill Clinton's personal life, but his 1992 campaign catchphrase, "It's the economy, stupid," hit the nail on the head: in the 1990s, the economy was booming. On Wall Street, the Mob was about to cash in. The bosses of the Five Families gave Frankie permission to cross Family lines and he recruited men from all of them. As Frankie's crew of upstart brokers mastered the techniques of cold calling, he'd get them on the phone to sell securities.

"I'd buy all different kinds of leads and they'd get on the phone and solicit business all day long. And every single one of them at the time was Kelly Scott. The pitch would go something like this:

"'Hi. My name is Kelly Scott and I'm a licensed stockbroker with Robert Todd Securities, located in downtown Manhattan. I'm a million-dollar manager and Bear Sterns is my holding company. What I'm basically doing today is giving a call to introduce our firm. Can I ask you what kind of stock you currently have, how large your portfolio is, and what your interests are?'"

Frankie's crew, because that's what they were, a white-collar crew, knew what they were doing wasn't kosher. Why else would each of them represent themselves on the phone as "Kelly Scott?"

"The idea is to get the guy on the phone, and get him to answer three or four questions about his portfolio. If he does that, he's a qualified lead. Then I would have four or five guys who would call back two days later with a great idea, an unbelievable opportunity that he can't pass up."

What made the deal work was the clearinghouse.

"The clearinghouse was basically an investment banking firm that's been around forever. It's what gives your firm legitimacy because they're the ones who actually hold the client's money—it would go through Bear Sterns first and then it would come to us."

The clearinghouse actually settles the trades and regulates delivery, which is the legal transfer of and receipt of ownership rights.

"The companies we recommended were legal companies, but they might have had some gray in their operations. We knew that; the client didn't. We sold everything with an extremely inflated commission, like a dollar a share. What wasn't legal was that we would hold the people into the stock. And here's how we did it.

"What we would do is take a string of tanning salons public, which we did with Fantastic Tan, and the clients and us [the Five Families] would buy in at the IPO [initial public offering]. Then what we would do is we'd rally the stock the first day.

"The IPO would be, say, five bucks, and we'd rally it on the boards to nineteen, twenty bucks a share. We did that by getting our people on the phone to sell 'em. Clients got so interested in the deal, they were lining up to buy it. 'Give me five thousand shares, give me twenty thousand shares,' they'd say. Then, with the stock price inflated with the client's legitimate money, we'd sell out at the top price. After that, we'd tell the client, 'You can't sell right now, you'll kill the deal.' We'd hold them in because they'd lose if they sold when the stock was in the dumper. But we'd have our money out at a tremendous profit."

Shortly after the clients had taken their bath and the stock was diving off the board, Frankie closed Robert Todd. "We took the furniture, the phone system—everything—and moved on." The clients couldn't come after him and the Securities and Exchange Commission (SEC) couldn't find him. "Then I went out and looked for another joint to get into. After Robert Todd I went into a place called First United. It was a firm a friend of mine was starting up with Ronnie One Arm, who was a Gambino.

"Once a legitimate firm, for whatever reason, lets one gangster in, you do nothing there anymore. You own the joint: your name is on the fucking door and you might sign the checks, but you don't do nothing else."

While there were a few Mob guys trying to pull the same type of scam, it was Frankie who perfected the system he used at Robert Todd in a way that no one could.

"When [wise]guys started to see the kind of money I was pulling out of these joints, they were rallying to get their hands on me to do the same for them."

Frankie was only too happy to oblige. He took what he could out of First United and went onto Jarrett Securities, Stratton Oakmont, and others. Most of the time he went into an established firm that had some sort of Mob presence already and then solidified the Mob's hold on it.

"At this point, I got maybe fifty, sixty guys in my crew. I wouldn't even bring my guys down to the firm. I would go rent a fucking warehouse, put forty, fifty desks in, put a phone system in it, and fax machines. I would have all my guys calling from the fucking warehouse and we'd be faxing the fucking trades over to the actual firm. This is where the term 'boiler room' comes from."

Every firm Frankie was involved with used Bear Sterns as its clearinghouse. The name of the broker on each buy and sell ticket was Kelly Scott. Frankie does not recall Bear Sterns ever questioning how Kelly Scott was able to sell such a phenomenal amount of securities, why it was that the IPOs he recommended always tanked, or why Scott, for all of his "success," kept moving from firm to firm.

"See, each firm would have a different manager's name. I would just put Kelly's name down as broker. I don't know if they knew what was happening. They loved the money, I'm sure. But eventually, they started turning a lot of our business down. They're not stupid," says Frankie.

It's hard for Frankie to figure out how much he sold in securities over the years, from 1992 to 1998 when he finally got out of the business. A conservative estimate would place the total stock sales of the firms he was involved with in the billions.

"I took out an average of anywhere from fifty to a hundred thousand a month for myself—and that's being moderate. It depended on what it was. On one deal I could take away two hundred and fifty thousand. And I'm kicking upstairs to the bosses. My kick up was always ten percent. I was averaging about a million and change a year."

As for where the money went, "I spent it like I made it buddy, believe me," Frankie says. "The suit guy would come to me once a month and I'd spend ten thousand with him for four suits. I was always picking up the check. Never ate nothin' but filet mignon and lobster; never drank nothin' but Crystal [champagne]."

Frankie never worried about being caught; he was always cautious. "Kelly Scott" was making the trades, not he. No where on paper did Frankie Saggio's name appear. He never worried that one of his "brokers" would spill the beans. What for? Frankie treated his crew well, just like his Uncle Philly had, paying them with hundreds of thousands of dollars in stock trade commissions.

By 1998, some of the legitimate brokers at Stratton Oakmont had come to think of themselves as wiseguys.

"The legit guys would kick up to the wiseguys, who were really running things. And they figured that they were in with them, they were part of the crew. So they started telling real wiseguys that they were with so and so. Their job, though, was to sell securities—not act like fucking gangsters. We started giving them fucking beatings to keep them in line—the managers, too.

"If the legit guys managing these firms gave us trouble, we slapped them around. If we had to fucking strangle them, we strangled them. If we had to kick them all over their office, we did that too. We did whatever we had to do."

But Frankie was not just making money off of stocks.

"I had a smokin' shylock business going in all these brokerages. My shylock business was fucking incredible! Guys would get a paycheck for fifty grand; two weeks later they'd be broke as a muthafucker. That's how stockbrokers are.

"When we would take a guy into our business, we'd tell him, 'You gotta make yourself make the money.' I wanted them to need money, to have an expensive lifestyle, so when they didn't—which was most of the time—I'd be there to shy 'em the money just to keep up."

Frankie even had his hooks into brokerages where he wasn't selling securities. On more than one occasion, he went into Paine Webber and Shearson Lehman to beat up brokers who were light on the vig. "No one stopped me because half of the guys in those places owed me too," Frankie says.

Things were going well, but the bubble had to burst. Either the legit brokers would get sick and tired of the wiseguys and try to get them out, or the SEC would begin investigating why Frankie's businesses opened and then closed with alarming frequency whenever the securities they sold went south. The brokers blinked first when the management of Stratton Oakmont became so scared of their Mob partners that they hired former NYC detective Bo Dietl to manage their personal security.

"Dietl didn't scare any of the wiseguys," Frankie claims. But things had started to get too hot. It was time to get out.

By that time, the bosses had to acknowledge that no one in the history of the Mob had ever mounted a criminal enterprise of such sheer brilliance. Frankie had done what no one ever had: he had crossed Family lines over and over with his multi-family crew and made money for all of them.

Every single Family—Lucchese, Bonanno, Columbo, Gambino, and Genovese—had guys on Frankie's crews kicking upstairs. Even with the artificially lowered estimates of profits that the wiseguys paid tax on, the bosses were still making millions. Frankie's stock schemes, in addition to a few others, enabled him to ascend the Outfit's ladder of economic prosperity.

Far and away, Frankie Saggio was the biggest earner in the Five Families. He had absorbed the essential business lesson from his uncle. But it overwhelmed the other one Philly Lucky had tried to teach him: "'Take care of your family, Frankie. Family's everything. Keep your family separate from your business,'" Frankie recalls his Uncle Philly saying.

Frankie's family now included his daughter Marina, who was born in 1988. Frankie wasn't there a lot when she grew up, not because he didn't want to be, he did, but because he had to make a living. He had to be out there on the street hustling, every hour of every day. The hustle was as addictive as any drug.

He kept his family separate from his business by never discussing business with his wife Anna. But Frankie, who is a careful, thoughtful listener, had misunderstood part of Uncle Philly's advice. When he advised

Frankie to take care of his family, he didn't just mean financially, he meant emotionally, too. Frankie did not understand that. He was too immature to realize that Phil Giaccone's greatest strength had been the love his family felt for him because he himself had loved them selflessly. Frankie had never committed a selfless act in his life.

Anna wanted a husband to love her and to come home to her bed at night. Instead, she got Frankie: a guy who was out at all hours making deals. "My weakness was never women," Frankie emphasizes, "just money. If it was on the table, I felt it was mine."

With that kind of self-centered attitude, it wasn't surprising that by the early 1990s, Frankie and Anna's marriage had started to crumble. Divorce is not an easy thing in a Catholic family. Unless the Church agrees to annul the marriage, the divorcés are excommunicated. In that sense, the religion is unforgiving. But Frankie and Anna took their chances and were divorced. Marina went to live with her mother, which meant Frankie saw her even less.

His Uncle Philly had killed men to obtain his position, Frankie knew that to be a fact. Killing was a way of life in the Outfit. No one who survived did so without clipping someone, or collaborating on a murder at one time or another. Such actions were important for maintaining respect and reputation. Yet strangely, Frankie declined to follow his uncle down that road. Somewhere in the back of his mind, Frankie always remembered what his uncle had said about never expecting to reach the age of fifty.

Frankie Saggio was next in line for becoming a made guy. The books were officially closed, but when they opened, Frankie Saggio was first on the list. He was determined to be the first inductee never to have killed anyone.

It really was an amazing record: ten years in the Mob and no kills to his credit. Frankie could hardly believe it himself. For all the times he had carried a gun and for all of the crazy animals he had dealt with, he'd never had to clip anybody.

"That just wasn't my thing," he says. "Let Mikey or somebody else really use their muscle. Sure, I knocked guys around, but shoot 'em? How could I look my daughter in the eye and do that?"

To a fourth generation mobster like Frankie, becoming a made guy should have meant something special. In a way, it did. But Frankie was aware of how things had changed. It used to be that to be a made guy, someone officially inducted into the Mob through an elaborate ceremony you had to have a pure Italian bloodline. John Gotti had changed all that.

"Gotti made his son a made guy despite the fact that his mother, Gotti's wife, was Russian," says Frankie. "After that, guys started buying their way in. I know guys that paid 250K to become made guys. It was just so much bullshit."

After numerous unsuccessful prosecutions, the government finally got Gotti when he was convicted on Racketeer Influenced Corrupt Organizations Act (RICO) and other charges in 1990, and they sent him to prison for life, where he has since died.

"Most of the guys in the Mob were glad Gotti had gone away," Frankie confirms. "All he did was focus too much attention on their businesses. And with Gotti away, they we were freer to act."

Change was afoot in the Bonanno Family. Stricken with liver cancer, Rusty Rastelli was transferred to the Medical Center for Federal Prisoners in Springfield, MO. He was later sent back to New York and died on June 24, 1991, at Booth Hospital in Queens. Capo Big Joey Massino, who was convicted at the same time as Rastelli, had been released earlier for good behavior.

As part of the faction that had backed Rastelli in 1981 and conspired to have the three recalcitrant capos assassinated, Massino's loyalty and ferocity were finally rewarded when he ascended to the Bonanno Family's throne. Massino's first edict was for his street bosses to produce more.

Suddenly, the Bonannos turned their eye to their wayward son.

Chapter Seven

CHEVY CORVETTE CONVERTIBLE

F rankie didn't waste any time grieving over his failed relationship with Anna; she got the house in Dix Hills and he got his freedom.

"About the time I was getting divorced, Mikey Hollywood was seeing this girl," Frankie says. "Mikey was going to a bar called the Long Island Exchange, where he was meeting his girlfriend and a couple of other girls.

"'Frankie, there's this really pretty girl coming, you would probably like her. I could introduce you to her,' he told me. And that was where I met Aria for the first time.

"Aria was beautiful, intelligent, and sexy. She came from a good family that had no connection with any wiseguys, had graduated college with honors, and worked for NBC as a systems engineer. She had a good head on her shoulders—very intelligent. That night when we met, it was love at first sight—for me, anyway. We had a couple of drinks and hung out. I took her phone number and started taking her out. After a short time, we were inseparable. And basically that was it. I knew that I wanted to spend the rest of my life with her."

As for his profession, Frankie told Aria that he was a stockbroker, though she was hard-pressed to reconcile that fact with Frankie's fascination for armored cars.

"We'd go out on a date," Aria recalls, "to dinner and a movie, and whenever Frankie would see an armored car parked someplace, he'd have to stop and hang out. He loved to watch them unload their money.

"'Why do you always like this; why do you always like to watch that?' I'd ask him.

"'I don't know, it just interests me,' he'd say."

What interested Frankie was the problem the situation presented: how could he get all that money from the truck into his pocket? It wasn't that he intended to rob an armored car—that was stupid. He just loved the money.

"We used to stay out pretty late," Frankie recalls, "and we were pretty inseparable at the time. Matter-of-fact, one time I was at her house eating dinner with her and her family and I had a stickup to go to with Mikey Hollywood. He calls me up on the cell and I tried to blow him off.

"'Like, no way Frankie. Everything is ready: I got the car, I got everything. You got to meet me—boom, boom, and boom. It will only take a couple of hours and you can go back,' Mikey says.

"'Ah, we'll do it next week,' I said. I wouldn't talk specifics, obviously, because I'm sitting at the dinner table and people can hear me.

"'No, we got to do it now, now, now, now!' Mikey says.

"'Alright, I'll be right there,' I said. I hung up and turned to Aria. 'Look Hon, I got a deal that's falling apart unless I go now.'"

"I told him to go, the dinner could wait," says Aria. "He had a stock deal on the fritz and he had to fix it."

Frankie continues. "So I go and I meet Mikey. We stuck up some dope dealer for, like, I think we got twenty-five pounds of weed, sixty, seventy in cash maybe, and, like, a pound of coke or whatever. I forget exact amounts. Then I came back three hours later."

"I asked Frankie how the deal went," says Aria. "He said, 'Fine,' and he went downstairs to watch TV with my father. Actually, I knew Mikey; he always was a gentleman and polite."

It was Mikey who once again acted as best man at Frankie's second wedding to Aria on September 3, 1997.

Over the first year of their marriage, Aria began to catch on that her husband wasn't some ordinary broker. One too many late nights got Aria thinking that Frankie had a girl on the side. But she could find no evidence and besides, he never seemed to have that kind of roving eye.

"I'll tell you how I finally figured out what he was," she says. "We're in the car and Frankie stops for gas and the whole time we're driving, something is rolling around under my feet. It's dark so I can't see 'til we get under the light of the gas station. I reach under the driver side seat and I feel something. I pull out a ski mask and duct tape. And it's *July*."

Frankie was just getting out of the stock business at the time and still had a brokerage he was attached to in the city. When he got home that day, Aria confronted him.

"'What the fuck is this?' I said to him. He tried to bullshit me, but it wouldn't work. I was smarter than he was."

Frankie recalls how he responded to Aria's question. "'The ski mask? We used it to stick up some low-life drug dealin' pieces of shit who sell drugs to kids,' I finally confessed. I figured if I put it that way, she wouldn't go that crazy. She hated drugs and dealers.

"'We?' she asked.

"'Me and Mikey Hollywood.'

"'And the tape? What do you do? Tie 'em up with it?'

"I don't remember if I said 'Yes' or not."

In her head, Aria started replaying events: the cell phone conversations she overheard, the late-night dates, and the difficulty she had trying to see Frankie during the day. What she remembered in particular were his bruised knuckles.

"He'd come home one day and they were bruised and I could see they had been bleeding. What was a stockbroker who sits on his ass all day doing with bruised knuckles?

"'I hurt them moving something,' Frankie said.

"'You're in the Mob aren't you?' I finally said to him, and he didn't deny it. He just nodded.

"I realized that whole Mob thing was a part of him. I already had an idea Frankie might be doing something illegal because he'd get all these cell phone calls from Mikey and other guys. Now Mikey, I liked him; he was polite and he had a real job—sort of, anyway—as a delegate in the painters' union. But there was something a little off about him."

Aria was deeply in love with her husband and decided to stay with Frankie. She couldn't really figure out why; it was just that she was raised to think a marriage was for life, and that you took the good with the bad. That didn't mean, though, she had to accept his "profession."

She encouraged Frankie to start investing his money in legitimate businesses. Her hope was that by doing so, she could gradually turn him away from the wiseguys. Since they both loved food, her first suggestion was that he buy a restaurant.

"So I bought one," Frankie says. "It was on the water in Centreport—the Porto Mare Ristorante. The selling price was seven hundred fifty thousand. I bought the restaurant for three hundred seventy-five thousand cash. I went half with this guy Marco, who was in there already."

Actually, Frankie didn't pay Marco the money right away. He had it, but he wasn't going to dip into his own pocket for it when he could dip into someone else's.

"In other words, the guy lets me in the place with a promise of I'm going to give him three hundred seventy-five thousand within the next month. So me and Mikey start running a scheme. Basically, what it was is, in the restaurant we had a couple of different credit card merchant companies working for us—you know, the actual machine where you run the credit card through? We had three different machines. What that basically means is that you're processing credit cards through three different banks.

"So what happens is, I put together a network: guys who work in hotels, a woman who works for a clothes store in the mall, guys who work at car rental joints—anybody who takes credit cards. I got guys all over giving me credit card numbers. And as I'm getting the credit card numbers, I'm punching them into my little computer there, making it look like you had a party at my restaurant or that you had dinner at my restaurant. But it would always be a party because that was four or five thousand a clip. And I would get an approval code and then in two days, that money would be in my bank. I had a vice president at Chase Manhattan Bank and a vice president at European American Bank who would handle my accounts and transactions personally, and I'd take care of them. As soon as the funds from the credit card companies were available in my account, I'd pull out the cash and then put the money into a safety deposit box at another bank.

"A lot of them [the legitimate credit card holders] would protest. But what happened was, when I was getting numbers from the car rental places, right, they would have your driver's license number on a receipt with your social security number and your date of birth. So now you're calling to dispute, but I'm telling the credit card company, 'I'm sorry, but how could this guy dispute it? I looked at his driver's license, here is his driver's license number.' And there was no dispute then. Every other day I was picking up fifty to sixty thousand."

Using the money from the credit card scam, Frankie paid off his partner Marco in thirty days.

"What messed everything up was one of the car rental joints I was getting credit card numbers from was a U-Haul place that was right behind a police precinct. The cops used to rent from the joint. It was their numbers I was punching in.

"Now I'm getting captains and fucking cops all calling from the precinct saying, 'Hey, I never fucking spent five thousand in this joint.' And what happened was, eventually the bank froze my account with, like, sixty or seventy thousand in it. But they could only put a freeze on your account for twenty-four hours without any paperwork.

"In other words, they can verbally call the bank to put a freeze on your account. I had a guy at the time working in the bank—the vice president, who was on my payroll. He called me up at three-thirty in the afternoon.

"'Frankie, I got sixty thousand here,' he told me. 'The freeze is off. Come and grab it because tomorrow the freeze will go back on. I'll wait for you.'

"So I shot to the bank and he gave me my last sixty thousand and that was it. Then they froze my account. As for the credit card company, all they could do is sue the corporation for the money. Who gave a fuck? It wasn't my corporation. I just went in and changed the name of the joint. They can't do anything else. So I ended up putting, I don't know, maybe one million in charges through, out of which I ended up getting four hundred thousand in cash. The rest went to Mikey, Marco, and the kick to my skipper, Tough Tony, because at the time I was with the Genovese Family.

"Marco, on the other hand, Marco was with the Columbos and was part of Chubby Ideno's crew. What Marco—the fuckin' stupid zip—didn't know was that I'd known Chubby all my life. He'd been in my uncle's crew and after my Uncle Philly's death, Chubby fence-jumped and went over to Fat Patty Catalano's crew.

"Chubby was away but Marco, he was always telling me Chubby stories and all of this shit and everything. So I always told the kid, 'Keep your mouth shut and don't tell Chubby what you got or what you're doing or anything, because he'll swallow you up.' You know? Yeah, Chubby would swallow this kid up. He thought that all gangsters was friends and all kinds of shit and really, he didn't know much about anything, you know? And I told him, 'Just keep your mouth shut; don't brag about what you got or you're going to cause major problems here. We're going to have problems.' So of course, he didn't listen.

"One night I got to my restaurant and who is sitting at the bar? Patty Catalano, Chubby's skipper. And I know Patty is the primer. Yeah, he's coming because Chubby is getting out of jail, you understand? Chubby needs an income. Chubby needs a place that he can say he works at. He needs somebody to vouch for him. He needs money. That's why Patty is there. So there is Patty sitting there with his girlfriend.

"'Oh, how you doin' Frankie?' he says to me. 'Where you been, where you hanging out?' Patty's giving me the bullshit kisses before he fucks me. Then he gets to the point.

"'You know, Chubby is coming out of jail next week. We would like to have a little party for him here.' And Marco, my asshole partner, is sitting there telling him, 'Yeah, don't worry, we'll take care of it.'

"After Patty leaves, I tell Marco, 'You fucking idiot!' I didn't give a shit about the cost of the party, but I knew what comes with it is a headache because I'm with the Genovese and Patty Catalano was a Columbo. What was going to happen was the Columbos were going to say they were there in the first place because my partner Marco was with the Columbos before I stepped in. So now they got a legitimate beef to say that I stepped into their thing. Which is exactly what happened.

"They come for Chubby's party and the whole fucking top brass of the Colombo Family is there: the boss, Joe Waverly; the consigliere,

Ralphie Lombardi—who, incidentally, is a nice guy; all the capos, including Patty. So now I know I got a major fucking headache here.

"Now, when a guy gets out of jail, there's usually a celebration. I just happen to be the guy conned into doing it this time. You invite not only the guys in the Family of the guy coming out, you invite everyone else. So at Chubby's party you got guys from all the Families, including the Bonannos. Skin Camarada, my uncle's former bodyguard who called in sick the day he was shot, Skin's now a made member of the Bonannos and he's there.

"'Frankie, what you doin'?' Skin asks me.

"'I'm hanging around with Tough Tony from Parkside.'

"'You gotta come with us,' says Skin, 'us' meaning the Bonannos.

"'I like where I am,' I answered. Then a few weeks later, it happened to be a night that my mother was eating dinner there—you know, at the restaurant—when *he* showed up. See, a lot of the Bonanno action that goes on in the Island—matter-of-fact, almost *all* of the Bonanno action that goes on in the Island—Tommy D handles. So that's why Tommy D showed up.

"'Man, this guy has got some balls. After what happened at the wedding, he's showing up here all friendly like,'" my mother said to me."

What Tommy D saw was a fancy restaurant that sat six hundred, with a catering hall upstairs. Frankie knew that Tommy D liked what he saw. "It impressed Tommy. He saw a place pulling in a lot of fucking money. He saw dollar signs for the Family," says Frankie.

"He told me, 'You gotta be with us.'"

Tommy, though, wasn't just interested in the money. He wanted to own Frankie. He wanted to get Frankie back for spitting in his face at Philip's wedding; by Mob standards, that had been a grievous loss of face. Most of all, he wanted to keep a close eye on Frankie because he was Philly Lucky's nephew and he might still be planning revenge.

"Tommy was a raving paranoid, the kind of guy who asks the same question a hundred and fifty times and see conspiracies under every rock," Frankie says.

But to get Frankie back into the Bonanno Family would not be easy.

"There had to be a sit-down between the Genoveses and Bonannos to figure out where I belonged," Frankie remembers. "I had no choice."

It would be a sit-down between rival family capos. The place picked for the meeting was Tough Tony's Parkside Restaurant. For the bosses, the ransom was the biggest producer in the Five Families: Frankie Saggio.

For Frankie, the ransom was nothing less than his soul.

"I didn't want to go back with the Bonannos. I hated those guys—they'd killed my uncle. I wanted to stay with the Genoveses."

Frankie's criminal instincts were second to none. The fact that he wouldn't kill unless he had to made him even more dangerous. It meant his mind was clear to see from which way danger would come.

Marco's big mouth had started a lot of trouble. Before the big meeting could even take place, the Columbos asserted ownership of Frankie's restaurant since they had been there first through Marco. Frankie was relegated to silent partner.

"I was supposed to get about fourteen hundred a week. But after a few weeks I'd show up and Marco'd give me some bullshit story about not having the money. I wound up robbing the joint four times in a row. See, the guys back in the kitchen, they hated Marco and I used to treat them really nicely. So they'd see me at the back door knocking and every time they let me in. The third time, I gave them all a hundred dollar bill when I left," Frankie recalls, laughing. "But the last time, somebody called the cops. I got charged with robbing my own restaurant.

"A few months later, I buy into another place out near Kennedy Airport. Who do I see at the bar one night but that imbecile Marco. I lose my mind and I give him a beating; I'm kicking that muthafucker and what's Marco doin'? He's screaming for my wife.

"'Aria, Aria, help me!' My wife fucking hated him 'cause he was an idiot."

Marco would eventually slink his way back to the North Shore and the restaurant that he now owned outright. Unfortunately, Frankie and Aria had been correct in their analysis of Marco: if there was an award for "Stupidest Mobster of the Year," he would have won hands-down.

At his restaurant, Marco decided to pull the same kind of credit card scam that Frankie and Mikey had. Only Marco, in his infinite wisdom,

decided not to kick anything upstairs; he fig
know the difference. Marco was found in the w
with his throat slit.

In the Mob, extreme stupidity was punishabl

The day of the meeting, Frankie showed up earl

"'Don't worry kid, I'll do my best for you. Wh   go get some
White Castle and you and Mikey can wait together over in Spaghetti
Park,' Tony tells me. Mikey had come along to keep me company.

"'Come on, Frankie, let's get some burg,' Mikey says. And as I'm
leaving with him, I see Tommy arrive. He shakes Tony's hand and smiles
at me. And I hear him say as he walks in, 'This kid is Bonanno and has
always been.'

"Fuck him, I wanted to kill the muthafucker."

But Frankie couldn't do that, even if he wanted to.

"You don't clip a skipper or even talk that way unless you want to end
up buried on Boot Hill."

Instead, Frankie and Mikey waited in Spaghetti Park, anxiously
chomping their square burgers.

"I knew what was going on inside and knew it could take awhile. In
situations like this, where a guy's affiliation is in dispute, what the capos
do is go through your family tree—all of it. They trace your family back
as far as they can to figure out what family you should really belong to."

Frankie waited to see where his roots would lead him.

"I looked out at the old men playing bocci and thought about what
Tony always said: 'This life we have chosen is all bullshit, Frankie. But
you know, it's a lifetime marriage.'"

Chapter Eight

CHEVY CORVETTE CONVERTIBLE

T he first part of the discussion between the rival capos Tough Tony from the Genovese Family and Tommy D from the Bonanno Family centered on Philly Lucky.

Despite the fact that the Commission had sanctioned his assassination—only the Commission could authorize the death of a capo—and despite the fact that he had been officially disgraced within the Bonanno Family, Philly Lucky, in death, was *still a Bonanno*.

"Think of it," Frankie says. "The sons of bitches had killed him, chopped his body up. And they still owned him and his family. That was the beauty of the Outfit: once you were in, they owned you and yours for generations."

Which meant it looked like Tommy D had won before the contest even began. And Tough Tony? Tony knew Frankie had held back on the kick with the brokerages. He didn't care; there'd been enough to go around for everyone. Frankie had said he would make money for everybody and he had kept his word.

The conversation would then have turned to Frankie's great-uncle Suvio Grimaldi. Suvio was Castellammarese. He had crossed the Atlantic in the early part of the twentieth century during the same wave of immigration that had brought Salvatore Maranzano and Joe Bonanno to the United States. Maranzano had worked his way up the criminal chain, and became one of New York's two big crime bosses; the other was Joseph Masseria. Both were eventually assassinated by men in the employ of Lucky Luciano, who would go on to create the Five Families with Bugsy Siegel and Meyer Lansky.

Joseph Bonanno worked his way up the ladder from soldier to boss and eventually ran his own Family. During the 1960s, Bonanno attempted a power play in order to become the most powerful Mafia boss—and lost. He was forced into an early retirement in Arizona where he died in 2002.

And Suvio? He became part of the Profaci Family, which would later be renamed the Columbo Family. Suvio married a woman named Octavia Glaizzo; she had a brother, Joseph.

"My grandfather Joseph was a handsome man with dark hair," recalls Petrina Saggio. "He was stocky and a sharp dresser. My grandfather had a ride, a portable whip."

During the summer in Brooklyn, a man would drive a trailer around. Attached to the trailer was a multiarmed octopus that whirled around with terrific centrifugal force. Kids would pay him a nickel and hop in for the ride. Joseph Glaizzo was the gentle man whose fingers were on the ride's power control.

"He also had an ice business. He carried the ice up the steps into people's homes when they still had iceboxes. He wasn't emotionally demonstrative to my grandmother, but he was a good man," Petrina says.

In 1932, Joseph's brother-in-law Suvio, later Frankie's maternal great-uncle, was charged with illegal possession of firearms. Suvio, however, wasn't about to go to jail.

Petrina recounts Suvio's craftiness. "Suvio told his brother-in-law Joseph, 'Look Joe, if I'm convicted, I'll get a long sentence.' My grandfather asked him why.

"'Because I got a record. I'll get a long sentence. But you, Joe, you got no record. You take the rap; you'll be out a year—two, tops.' My grandmother, she loved her brother Suvio, so my grandfather did it for her."

And that's how an innocent, good man named Joseph Glaizzo plead guilty to a crime he did not commit and served two years in the same state prison system that would house his great-grandson. In manipulating the situation, Suvio showed that he had mastered the real lesson of the gangster's trade: survival. And Joseph?

Frankie says, "When I heard that story about my great-grandfather

Joseph, I thought, 'This guy has got balls. A stand-up guy!' Later I real-ized he'd been duped too. But by that time there was no way out."

Suvio Grimaldi gave Frankie his first tie to the Profaci/Columbo Family. His Uncle Jimmy Clemenza gave him his second. Outside in Spaghetti Park, Frankie was thinking of his Uncle Jimmy too. He knew Tony was going to mention Suvio and Jimmy; they were his only chance to stay clear of the Bonannos. He didn't want to be put into a situation where he had to constantly be watching his back.

As Frankie waited in the park, he remembered the story the Saggio family told about the one time Uncle Jimmy went to kill somebody and things didn't go right. It was such a famous story that Francis Ford Coppola and Mario Puzo used it for the pivotal scene in *The Godfather, Part II*. . . .

The Corleone Family has a disgruntled, old-line capo named Frankie "Five Angels" Pantangelo. He hates "those pimps the Rissoto Brothers," who have no respect and are butching in on his action. He goes to the Don, Michael Corleone, to ask permission to kill them, but Michael refuses. He's too involved in other business deals with Hyman Roth to want the attention that would result from the Rissoto Brothers' assassi-nations.

Shortly after Michael turns down his request, Frankie Five Angels is in a bar back in New York when two guys come in and try to garrote him. They have the piano wire wound tightly around his throat and are squeezing the life out of him when a cop stumbles in and sees what's happening. Before he can react, the two assassins gun him down and flee. Frankie Five Angels recovers, thinks it was Michael who arranged his death, and decides to testify against him before a Senate committee that is looking into organized crime.

Michael eventually discovers that it was Hyman Roth who planned Frankie Five Angels's assassination. Through a series of deft maneuvers, not only does Frankie Five Angels fail to implicate Michael, he absolves him of any criminal responsibility. He then conveniently takes his own life, which seals his lips forever. Michael is left to rule his criminal empire unimpaired.

• • •

The actual story has none of the movie's glamour, but the real drama.

During the Depression, James "Jimmy Brown" Clemenza was a gangster. He wasn't some newspaper hound like Baby Face Nelson, Pretty
Boy Floyd, or Bonnie and Clyde, the gangsters who robbed and killed
for kicks and headlines. Jimmy was in it for the money: he did his job
without the headlines.

To Clemenza and the professional thieves and murderers in the Mob,
headlines meant attention; attention meant cops; cops meant prison.
Prison was a fate to be avoided if possible—and it was always possible.

Jimmy bootlegged quietly in Cicero, a suburb of Chicago, with
another boy from the Brooklyn Mob named "Scarface" Al Capone.
While officially attached to what would become the Profaci Family,
Jimmy was on loan to Capone's Mob. When Prohibition was repealed in
1932, Jimmy came home to Brooklyn.

Over the next three decades he would do all kinds of jobs for the Profaci Family. Jimmy Brown had served the Profaci Family faithfully since
its inception and he would continue to do so until he died. He was a true
old-liner, a skipper who believed in keeping your word and your place,
which is why he watched with distaste as the Gallo Brothers kept trying
to butch in on the Profaci's action.

Throughout the 1950s, Larry Gallo, Joseph "Crazy Joe" Gallo, and
their youngest brother, Albert "Kid Blast" Gallo, worked as assassins for
Nicholas "Jiggs" Forlano. The New York State Commission of Investigation would later identify Forlano, a member of the Profaci Family, as
the biggest loan shark in New York City.

The Gallo Brothers got tired of waiting to move up the Mob ladder.
In 1959, they formed their own gang of about twenty with guys in the
Profaci Family who were equally dissatisfied with Profaci's leadership.
While Crazy Joe was the one to be feared in any encounter—he had
been certified as insane by a psychiatrist at Brooklyn's Kings County
Hospital in 1950—it was Larry who was the brains. If Larry were out
of the way, Joey, Kid Blast, and the rest would fall into the gutter.

Before anything like that could happen, the Gallos, with their ranks swelling to one hundred disaffected, got some of their guys to kidnap four of Profaci's closest advisers. Held for ransom, they were eventually released. Profaci then convinced most of the one hundred insurgents to come back into the fold. The Gallos, though, were a different story. Profaci believed they deserved retribution for the rebellion they had fomented.

The neighborhood was Flatbush, a mostly Jewish area of Brooklyn. A few Italians lived there too, in real middle-class splendor. Flatbush was a step up from Bensonhurst.

There were fewer attached four-family houses there; Flatbush had mostly semi-detached twos and stand-alone singles. One of the main access roads to the neighborhood that gangster Larry Gallo walked on was Eastern Parkway, the sedate, tree-lined street designed back in the early part of the century by the famed architect Frederick Olmsted, the same man who designed Central Park.

On August 25, 1961, Larry Gallo went to the Sahara Restaurant—a tavern that served only wine and beer—on Utica Avenue, a busy shopping street in the heart of Flatbush. In the dark interior, Larry lounged at the bar over his Pabst Blue Ribbon draught. Outside and down the block, a white sedan pulled up to the curb. Still drinking in the tavern, Gallo had no idea it was there.

Inside the sedan were three men: Frankie's uncle Jimmy and his brother Peter Clemenza, and an associate named John Scimone. Jimmy Clemenza got out of the car and quietly walked down the street. He approached the Sahara steadily but warily, making sure there were no cops around, no witnesses. Then, he turned and quickly walked in the door, his porkpie slouch hat covering his face.

Gallo was swallowing some of the beer when a rope wound around his throat; one moment it wasn't there and the next, it was. As Gallo reached up to try and pull it off, the person holding it, Jimmy Clemenza, pulled harder and the fibers of the rope sunk deeper into Larry Gallo's flesh.

Gallo knew he was being garroted. He knew the action had to have been ordered by the Profacis, with the Commission signing off on the assassination. He also knew there wasn't much he could do. The person strangling him—he still didn't know who it was—had incredibly strong hands. Despite his struggles, he was dying.

Clemenza was literally choking the life out of Gallo. He knew from having done it before that Larry Gallo would stay conscious for at least the first minute and a half. Then Gallo's brain would suffer oxygen deprivation and he'd black out. Until then, it would be sheer, unrelenting agony. Even when Gallo went limp in his hands, Clemenza would know he was unconscious, but not dead. If he stopped strangling him at that point, there was a possibility that Gallo could be revived. Clemenza would keep up the pressure until he heard his hyoid or throat bone crack and than apply still more pressure until Gallo was clearly, definitely, absolutely dead.

Larry Gallo was just on the verge of passing out when Sergeant Edward Meagher stumbled onto the scene. Meagher had been in a radio car at 2:45 P.M. with Patrolman Melvin Biel when he decided to go into the tavern for a "routine inspection." Jimmy Clemenza, seeing Meagher coming in, dropped Gallo to the floor and hid.

When Meagher got inside, it took a second for his eyes to adjust to the gloom. Then he saw a man lying motionless on the dirty floor and heard him groaning. Meagher crossed the room and bent down to assess the man's condition. Just then, Jimmy Clemenza raced out of the shadows to the waiting getaway car.

Outside, Biel saw Clemenza running and gave chase. Clemenza turned and ran up the street. The white sedan, the getaway car, followed. Someone inside the car, either Peter Clemenza or Scimone, stuck a revolver out of a window and fired a shot that hit Biel on the right cheek. Jimmy Clemenza jerked open the car door and hustled inside. For a man who weighed over 250 pounds, he moved quickly when he had to.

Hearing the shots, Meagher fled the bar, saw the automobile escaping, pulled his service revolver, and fired two shots as the sedan turned north on Utica Avenue and sped north. He didn't hit anything.

Four blocks away, at the intersection of Snyder Avenue and East 49th Street, the sedan slowed down. As bystanders watched in surprise, John Scimone was pushed out of the car and unceremoniously hit the street. Apparently, the Clemenzas felt he was expendable. Scimone, who had been arrested thirty years before for assault and robbery, made a good patsy: he could be blamed for the attempted murder.

Larry Gallo survived, though his voice was a little hoarse after that. As for Jimmy Brown, it was the only time he failed to clip someone. No one held it against him, however; it was just dumb luck that the cop showed up. By the following year, Jimmy Brown once again had to adjust to changing times.

On June 6, 1962, the twenty-eighth anniversary of D-Day, Joseph Profaci died in the South Side Hospital on Long Island. The cause of death was cancer. There is always an immediate rush to fill the vacuum created whenever a family head dies. But Profaci had no heirs. His brother-in-law, Giuseppe Magliocco, stepped up to fill his shoes and assumed control of the family enterprises.

Looking on with a gleam in his criminal eye was boss Joe Bonanno. Profaci had been his close friend. Nevertheless, his death gave Bonanno an unbelievable opportunity to become the most powerful crime boss since Maranzano. Bonanno devised a scheme that involved clipping family heads Carlo Gambino and Tommy Lucchese and Tommy's cousin, Buffalo, NY family boss Stefano Maggadino. Unfortunately, Bonanno was relying on the young capo Joseph Colombo to take care of the killings.

Columbo was actually in tight with Carlo Gambino. He looked at Gambino like a father; he would never betray him. When Gambino found out from Columbo about Bonanno's scheme, he called the Commission into session. Bonanno was asked to explain himself. The deceitful boss was able to talk his way out of having his body carved up and distributed throughout the New York Metropolitan area and retired to Arizona in the late 1960s.

As for Columbo, with Gambino's backing, he became head of the old Profaci Family, newly christened the Columbo Family. Jimmy Clemenza would continue to do jobs as demanded by his Family and also become a capo until he retired to Florida in the late 1970s.

"My Uncles Jimmy and Philly bought in Hallandale [Florida] in 1978," says Frankie. "The building was all Italian and Jewish gangsters—

funniest thing you ever saw. They would argue day and night. They had a clubhouse where they played cards. All they did was make Hallandale into Brooklyn. They'd been playing cards back home in New York for thirty years.

"Let's see, who else was there from New York? Scottie DiAngelo; Joe Sausage, who owns GS Sausage in Jersey; Angelo Ponti, who owns Ponti Carting. He just went away on extortion. My Uncle Jimmy used to curse every one of them.

"I remember standing in a parking lot talking to Scotty DiAngelo. I'm eighteen or nineteen and these condos all have catwalks and my uncle yells down, 'What you doin' talking to that cheap bastard?' I was embarrassed. I couldn't understand why Scotty's name was 'Scotty' until someone explained 'Scotty' means 'cheap' in Italian."

Besides Hallandale, Clemenza had a home in Florida, NY, where he raised horses. When Jimmy wasn't at home either at the farm or at the Florida condo, he could usually be found in North Carolina.

"Uncle Jimmy used to go to Duke University in North Carolina for the Rice Diet," Frankie says. "He was a big guy—really fat—and he needed to lose weight."

Lina Saggio, Frankie's sister, takes up the story.

"My cousin Corinne told me about the Rice Diet. She said that Uncle Jimmy went down there for years to lose weight. 'Boy I'd love for you to go,' she said. I needed to lose some weight then, so I went down in 1984 with the agreement that my Uncle Jimmy was there and he'd take care of me.

"'You're here to do one thing and one thing only: You're going to lose weight and forget about anything else,' Uncle Jimmy said to me as soon as I got off the plane. He was heavy and had a rough voice from all the cigars he smoked. He said whatever he felt like and you just had to take it.

"We stayed at a hotel where he was head honcho. Every day he took my arm and we'd have to walk eight miles a day to get our meals. He had a driver down there too and him and the driver would follow me with the Caddy, to make sure nothing happened.

"Uncle Jimmy, he was respected everywhere. Even when he was

doing the diet and went in the hospital to give blood and urine samples, it was always 'Good morning, Mr. Clemenza,' 'How ya doin' Mr. Clemenza,' from the staff."

But even Jimmy Clemenza's considerable influence was not enough to stop love from blooming.

"What happened was, he used to watch me from his window when I'd go out. He was afraid I'd go and eat something or meet the wrong kind of person. One day, I met my husband-to-be, Kelly Scott, at a convenience store next door to the hotel. I was there buying cigarettes and started talking to him.

"'Come to the hotel and have lunch,' I suggested.

"'OK, I'll come over,' he said. When he walked in the front door, he was stopped by Uncle Jimmy.

"'You go in the dining room,' Uncle Jimmy told me. But I stayed to listen.

"'Do you know who I am?' he asked Kelly.

"'No,' Kelly answered.

"'This is my niece. Leave her alone and stay away from her.'

"'I like her and I think she's nice,' Kelly said.

"'See the leather on your shoes? Keep walking,' said Uncle Jimmy and his chauffeur escorted Kelly out.

"I was crying. I called up my father. He talked to Uncle Jimmy. My father told Uncle Jimmy not to hurt him. My brother, he talked to Uncle Jimmy and got him to cool off and leave me alone. But Uncle Jimmy was still giving Kelly the business so a couple of days later, I took off with Kelly and left Uncle Jimmy behind."

Eventually, Lina married Kelly and her family accepted him as one of their own. A few years later, Uncle Jimmy died a peaceful, natural death. He had managed to live his life the way he wanted: as a true outlaw who, in the end, died in bed. But Uncle Jimmy also knew he was one of the few who actually fulfilled such a wish.

After carefully evaluating all of Frankie's family tree, Tommy D and Tough Tony came to the conclusion that, if anywhere, Frankie belonged with the Columbos. Two of his uncles had been in that Family compared with only one in the Bonanno Family. But the Columbos did not have a representative at the sit-down and a Bonanno and Genovese were not about to give the Columbos the Five Families' prime earner.

Tough Tony was forced to admit that he held the losing hand; there was no blood relationship between the Genovese and Frankie. Tony had just taken him in, while Tommy and the Bonannos could show a direct link to Frankie Saggio through Philip Giaccone.

From across the street, Frankie watched as the door to the Parkside Restaurant opened and Tony emerged, grim-faced. Frankie hoped that Tony had won and was just putting on an act for Tommy's benefit. Frankie remembers how Tony broke the news.

"'You belong with the Bonannos, kid. There's nothing I could do,' Tony told me. Tony felt bad. He knew how much I hated Tommy D. I was being forced to go back to work with the crew that killed my Uncle Philly."

And now, Frankie Saggio really needed to start watching his back.

PART THREE: THE FUGITIVE

Chapter Nine

EL DORADO, LINCOLN TOWNE CAR

Just because he was back with the Bonannos, it didn't mean that Frankie couldn't do business with guys outside the Family; his "passport" had been stamped.

Frankie was gold. He could run scams with anyone he wanted, across all the Family lines. He had achieved the goal he had set for himself after his Uncle Philly died almost twenty years before: he was barely into his thirties and he was a Mob veteran entering his third decade as a wiseguy.

And at the same time, he had failed. He wasn't the independent he had set out to be. Worse, he had been naïve enough to believe that if he were the biggest earner, the bosses would have no choice but to give him his freedom. Well, he had indeed become the biggest earner in the Mob and where had that gotten him? Right back with the Bonannos. Instead of Tough Tony and the Genovese he was kicking upstairs to Tommy D, who was now his capo in the Bonanno Family.

"Tommy doesn't believe in paying for nuthin'," says Frankie. "Angelo's, the restaurant on Route 219, he eats there because he doesn't get a check. Tommy killed a guy at White Castle and beat a guy to death in a parking lot."

Frankie knew every scumbag grifter, thief, robber, sadist, killer, and serial killer in the Mob and nobody—*nobody*—was as bad as Tommy D.

"Listen to this. He's got a moron for a son. Tommy Jr. decides to run a scam where girls would call up guys to get them to buy stuff. So he says to me, 'I got these beautiful girls to do it.'

"'Tommy,' I said, 'what difference does it make if they're beautiful or

not? You want girls who give good phone. No one can see them, right?'
He thinks for a second and then says, 'Oh yeah.' This is what I had to
deal with."

Frankie's hatred toward the Bonannos for killing his uncle was in
direct proportion to the respect he had for Tough Tony. He missed the
days sitting and eating White Castles in Spaghetti Park with the intro-
spective capo. Instead, he was stuck with Tommy. Though his new relationship with Tommy gave him agita, his relationship with his wife, Aria,
was the saving grace in his life.

"I kept telling Frankie that he needed to find a way out," says Aria.
"He was smarter than these guys he did business with. I knew if he could
find some other business to get into, maybe that would be the way out."

Aria did not come from a Mob family. No matter what she thought
she knew, the one thing she could not appreciate was that Frankie, just
like his uncles, was in for a life hitch. The only way out was feet first.
Maybe it's this inevitability in the lives of mobsters that makes them
enjoy food so much, and tobacco, liquor, sex—all the creature comforts.
They enjoy what they can when they can because they know intuitively
that it all will probably end in the back of a Caddy with a bullet in the
head. Weddings, christenings, parties of all kinds, have always been extra
special occasions for mobsters—they may not be around to see another.

Frankie and Aria got invited to a particularly festive wedding in 1998.

"Our friend Mickey D [Michael DeLucia] was getting married. Jesse
Burke was one of the guests. You remember in *Goodfellas*, Robert
DeNiro played Jimmy Burke, the Irish gangster? Well, I knew Jimmy
very well from the airport. Jimmy had two sons who he named Frank
James Burke and Jesse James Burke. Jimmy thought that was very
funny."

Jimmy, of course, had no sense of history. The real Jesse James had
been assassinated by Bob Ford, a member of his own gang. Ford shot the
outlaw in the back while he was hanging a painting in his house in 1881.
It never occurred to Jimmy that the same thing could happen to his son.
Or maybe he just didn't care.

The business of the Mob was business, and so it was after the DeLucia
wedding. On Monday, it was back to thievery as usual. Frankie was about

to go into business with a modern-day Bugsy Siegel, a gangster/entrepreneur who wanted to be a movie producer. His name was Robert Misseri. Misseri was a protégé of the famous Columbo Family capo Sonny Franzese, who is a living legend. Sonny came up as a soldier in the Columbo Family in the 1960s, shortly after Philly Lucky became a made member of the Bonannos. They knew each other.

Whereas Philly Lucky's cover for his Mob activities was his trucking business, Franzese's was in the record business. He had a connection with Buddah Records, a big label that put out the Isley Brothers and other great artists in the 1960s. Franzese had branched out into films and supposedly had a piece of the Linda Lovelace porn classic, *Deep Throat*.

Sonny was also a major player during the Gallo Brothers' revolt. He seemed to have it all in place to rise to the top. And then, as quickly as it had come, it all started to crash down. Franzese was convicted of being behind a series of bank robberies and got a fifty-year sentence.

He got out on an appeal and wasted not time in getting back to business. No sooner was he on the street, however, than he was charged with ordering the murder of some low-level wiseguy wannabe. Sonny seemed to have developed a tendency to get in trouble with the law—definitely not a good thing for a mobster. But Sonny was the one gangster with a certain *je ne sais quoi.*

Sonny was a survivor; he was never convicted of the murder. As a result, even with his conviction on the bank robberies, he'd eventually be up for parole. While Franzese served his sentence, boss Joe Columbo had a brainstorm. He decided to flaunt Mob convention and reinvent himself. Showing a marked absence of common sense, he formed the Italian American Civil Rights League, which was essentially the public relations and lobbying arm for the Five Families.

During 1969, 1970, and part of 1971, the Joe Columbo-run League events drew huge media coverage. If you turned on Channel 7 in New York, there was Peter Jennings, a local anchor before he went network, interviewing Joe. On Channel 2 the rugged anchor Jim Jensen posed the questions, while over on Channel 4, the intrepid Gabe Pressman went after the real story.

The Italian American Civil Rights League had one point it made over and over. You just had to ask Joe and he'd tell you on the record, on camera, at midnight kissing your ass in Macy's window—wherever: "Just because my name is Italian doesn't mean I'm in the Mob. That is discrimination."

In trying to get all Italians to support him, Columbo had limited success. He had forgotten that the same people from whom he was asking for help—the people he thought were his compatriots—actually hated his guts. The simple fact was that the majority of Italians were not in the Mob; they were hard-working people who resented his trying to rip them off with his rackets. And they weren't all that sorry when, under Commission orders, a gunman shot Joe Columbo in broad daylight at a 1971 Columbus Day rally at New York City's Columbus Circle.

If it had worked, it would have been the most spectacular assassination ever pulled off by the Outfit because the rally was being covered by national television. All the network evening news anchors—Walter Cronkite at CBS, Chet Huntley and David Brinkley at NBC, and Howard K. Smith at ABC—ran footage of the shooting. Unfortunately, Joe became the butt of a cruel joke that only a true Brooklynite could get the answer to:

Q: What's the newest Italian vegetable?
A: Joe Columbo.

Like Robert Kennedy a mere three years before, he was felled by an assassin's bullet. Joe, however, was stronger. He lived. The doctors bought him a few more wretched years as a human being with brain waves and little else.

Columbo capo Carmine Persico made a play for power. With Sonny away, Persico ascended the Mob ladder and became the Columbo Family boss. That still didn't stop Sonny from trying to butch in.

Over the next twenty years, Sonny was released on parole four times. Each time he was out he would violate the conditions of his strict parole, usually by associating with known wiseguys. It was during one of Sonny's times out on parole in 1998 that Frankie was pulled in on one of his music deals. By then, the Columbo Family soldier was eighty-one years old. Franzese was still as tough and deadly as ever; physically, he could kill a man swiftly when he had to.

"There was this meeting down in Marilou's. Sonny Franzese went down there to see them [music executives] over some business. Sonny's had a very strong hold on the music business for many years. Always did. I went down with him, his son Johnny, and other people. Johnny was getting involved with rap groups. And Sonny meets with these music guys.

"Everybody thinks these rappers are running things. They weren't. Every one of them [the music executives] is kicking upstairs to some wiseguy someplace along the line.

"'This is the way it's gonna be,' Sonny tells them."

Among the music executives at the meeting that night was Marion "Suge" Knight. Knight is the president of the premier hip-hop label, Death Row Records. Knight, who has a reputation as a two-fisted businessman, would later serve five years of a nine-year sentence on assault-related charges.

"'My kid wants to do anything, you don't interfere,' Sonny told them. 'My kid gets everything.' Looking straight at Knight, Sonny said, 'You interfere and you're going to have a serious headache a couple of Tylenol ain't gonna clear up.'"

Frankie found Knight a wannabe.

"He was a fat, well-dressed jerk-off who thought he was a gangster until he got put in his place by a guy who would have buried him right there if he said the wrong thing—and Sonny would have."

Which all leads back to Sonny's protégé, Robert Misseri.

"It was Tommy, through Sonny, that introduced me to Robert. 'I think you and this kid will make a fucking ton of cash together,' Tommy said.

"I had heard the stories about Robert, that he was a good guy, he wasn't a pushover. The kid was amazing and I have to tell you—because I can talk—this kid was amazing with his fucking mouth. He'd talk you out of your fucking underwear in three seconds. Robert wanted to get into the movie business. Robert had a company he was involved with called Vice Versa Films."

Frankie remembers Vice Versa producing programming for the Food Channel. The Food Channel describes itself this way:

> FOOD NETWORK is the nation's only 24-hour cable television network dedicated to good food and good times. With headquarters in New York City and offices in Atlanta, Los Angeles, Chicago, Detroit and Knoxville, FOOD NETWORK is distributed to more than 66 million U.S. households. Internationally, FOOD NETWORK programming is seen in Canada, Australia, France, Republic of Korea and the Philippines. The E.W. Scripps Company (NYSE: SSP), which also owns and operates Home & Garden Television Network (HGTV), Do It Yourself (DIY) and Fine Living, is the managing general partner.

In other words, the E.W. Scripps Company was unknowingly in business with Misseri, a man who would later be identified in a federal indictment as an alleged member of organized crime.

"We were going to eat at Patsy's on 57th [in Manhattan] and we stopped at a newsstand and bought a magazine. It was either *Variety* or the *Hollywood Reporter*, I'm not sure which. Robert showed me this picture inside of him. The caption identified him as one of the hottest new up-and-coming film producers in New York.

"Robert really wanted to get into the movie business. He wanted to option Jerry Capeci's book, *Murder Machine*, which was about the Roy DeMeo crew. Then he was going to get Abel Ferrara to direct the film. Abel used to hang around Marilou's."

Ferrara was the kind of guy who could make Capeci's compelling book into an equally fascinating film. The Bronx-born Ferrara's film credits included the critically acclaimed *Bad Lieutenant* that starred Harvey Keitel and *The King of New York* with Christopher Walken.

"I hosted a dinner at the Old Homestead Steak House with Robert, me, and Abel Ferrara. The idea was for Robert to convince him to direct. But you know what happened? The guy eats and eats at dinner, drinks Crystal champagne, and then without a word, when he's finished licking his chops, he gets up and walks out. I have no fucking idea where he went."

Misseri never got the option and Ferrara never got the gig. That didn't stop Misseri. Besides Vice Versa, he had other interests.

"When Robert and I got involved, at the time Robert had a company called Fast Cash for cars. He also had a car auction on Long Island with Michael DeLucia. We became partners and opened a company called American Pay Telephone."

What American Paytel did, according to an indictment later filed in United States District Court, Eastern District of New York, was—to put it mildly—illegal. That indictment would read:

> It was part of the scheme and artifice that the defendant FRANK SAGGIO, together with others, placed advertisements in publications, including "Pennysaver," that were delivered by United States mail. These advertisements solicited individuals to purchase pay-phones from American Paytel, as well as location, known as "routes," from which these payphones could be operated and promised profits to individuals from the operation, when, as the defendant FRANK SAGGIO well knew and believed, he and other participants in the scheme did not intend to deliver payphones and routes to these individuals.

Frankie's phony payphone routes were another million-dollar scheme for the Outfit. It was interesting how what was essentially a case of a very clever con job was elevated to the status of a federal crime and thus broke one of Philly Lucky's cardinal edicts: don't ever do anything that would bring the Feds looking for you.

The fact that Frankie advertised American Paytel in *Newsday*, the *Daily News*, the *New York Post*, *The New York Times*, and every other publication there was in the tri-state area more often than he did in *Pennysaver* made no difference to the Feds. Newspapers are not delivered by U.S. mail, except to subscribers. But everyone on Long Island received *Pennysaver* as part of their regular weekly mail.

In other words, Frankie was guilty of mail fraud, which made the business he did with American Paytel "customers" a federal crime. Eventually, there were over one hundred complaints against American Paytel filed by customers that the company had swindled. By that time, the Feds were courting Frankie.

"But I don't know that at the time," says Frankie. "They just kept watching me. Maybe I was into too many things at that point. Later, the [FBI] agents'd tell me how surprised they were at the places I was in, who I was with."

The Feds couldn't believe Frankie's ability to move between the Families—it was unheard of. As for Robert Misseri, he had a big mouth.

"Robert told me about this guy that he and a few other guys had clipped. He called him 'Cooler Boy' because they got rid of the body by pushing him into an ice cooler and dumping it in the ocean."

"Cooler Boy" was really thirty-year-old Louis P. Dorval of Nassau County, whom authorities would later identify as being involved with the Lucchese Crime Family. Dorval's body was found by a charter fishing boat off Fire Island in August 1994, the week after a federal indictment charged him and eight others in New Jersey as part of a drug and car theft ring.

What had happened, allegedly, was that Joseph "Joe the Blond" Pistone (not the Federal agent who masqueraded as Donnie Brasco, but a mobster who coincidentally had the same name), Robert Misseri, and a third, unidentified person put Dorval in a car where Pistone shot him several times. Pistone and Misseri then put Dorval's body into a cooler. Pistone and the unidentified person dumped the "full" cooler into the Atlantic Ocean, south of Long Island. The cooler later drifted back to shore and was discovered.

"Robert is really slick. Although physically I never thought much of him, he'd shoot you in a heartbeat. Out of all the guys I did business with, he was the sharpest," Frankie admits.

In the back of his mind Frankie knew that Misseri was someone to be reckoned with. His intelligence made him potentially a greater enemy than Tommy D. What Frankie didn't know was that the greatest enemy any mobster has—the government—was still on his tail.

The Feds had enough on Frankie to file an indictment against him in the pay phone scam. Enough of Frankie's fleeced customers had come forward to mount a compelling case. But they decided to wait until the time was right. With Frankie's connections, he could literally bring down all Five Families if they played their cards right. They just had to sit tight and wait for the opportunity.

By 1998, Frankie was still in the catbird's seat, spending money as fast as he made it. Aria wasn't too happy about that. What she really wanted was to have a family, but Frankie was always running here and there and there never seemed time. Besides, what kind of life could Frankie give a child? He loved his daughter and he saw her a lot, but it wasn't the same as being there all the time. Frankie missed a lot of Marina's growing up. And she still didn't know what he did for a living.

One night Frankie and Aria went out to dinner at a Suffolk County nightclub called The Vanderbuilt. "It was a wiseguy hangout," Frankie claims, and that particular evening there was a guy there, Sammy Forlani, from the Lucchese Family. He and Frankie had had words about something and neither was convinced that a satisfactory resolution had been rendered. But the dispute itself was unimportant. What happened next, was: "Forlani pulled a gun and started shooting," Frankie recalls. "Can you believe how stupid this guy was? In a nightclub filled with *civilians*, this stupid muthafucker starts shooting."

How did Frankie react?

"What was I supposed to do? Stand up and let him shoot me? My uncle didn't raise an idiot. I pushed my wife away and then I ducked behind this table. I waited until everyone was out of the way and then I pulled my Glock auto from behind my back and returned fire. The shooting stopped when Forlani ran out of bullets. I could have gone right over and shot the stupid muthafucker in the brain. But like I said, I'm not an idiot.

"'Aria, it's a good time to get the fuck out,' I turned and told my wife.

"She understood. I needed to get the hell out before the cops came. So I'm already out the door and the fucking bouncer yells, 'Freeze,' and with my back turned, he starts shooting. He had a gun too! This guy was like a fucking cowboy, pegging shots at me. My Corvette was parked in front of the place and it got hit with six bullets.

"When the cops [finally] came, they made my wife take the car out immediately because the bouncer was a fucking off-duty cop. They didn't want the department butching him for shooting in a crowded club."

"We were all lucky that no one was hit," Frankie continues. "But I wound up getting arrested. I was tried and convicted for carrying a concealed weapon. Normally you could plea bargain it down to a lesser charge, but I already had a record. I was sentenced to one year in the county lockup."

The Nassau "county lockup," or jail, is located in East Meadow. The jail there was filled with offenders getting ready for trial or those serving a limited sentence. The latter group was principally composed of guys serving a year or less on low-level misdemeanor and felony charges.

In this kind of a situation, there is a stereotype perpetuated by Hollywood movies and TV shows, as well as books written by mobsters that purport to "tell it like it really is": for the mobsters who keep their mouths shut and do their time, their families are taken care of while they are away.

That stereotype is about as realistic as *The Godfather, Part III*.

"I'm in jail and no one—*no one*—sends so much as a hundred bucks to my wife. Nobody offers a fucking quarter," Frankie reveals. "I'd call guys [from prison] and ask them to help my wife out and they'd say, 'Oh, I'm broke,' or 'I'm expecting a big score.' Those fucking lying cocksuckers."

Uncle Philly could have told Frankie that that would happen. The only thing Frankie could do now was serve his time.

Chapter Ten
DODGE DURANGO

Nassau County voters might be surprised to know that their county lockup tends to be a rather pleasant place to pass some time providing you have enough goods and services to bribe the guards. It was easy for Frankie to bribe the guards with cigars and fancy lighters so he was given special treatment that included gourmet meals. It was while he was in the county lockup, Frankie met a guy in the yard and they struck up a friendship.

"I'm away with this kid in jail, Andy Mayfair, who has an adult book-store. When I get out, he calls me and says, 'Frankie, these guys are shaking me down. I know you're hooked up, can you help me out?' I told him I'd talk to my guy and see what I could do."

Frankie's guy, of course, is Tommy D. So Frankie went to see him.

"Turned out the guy shaking him down was a Lucchese named Richie Capaldo. Tommy played poker with him every week. So he squares it with Richie and then sits down with this kid Mayfair.

"'I don't come cheap. It's four to five hundred a week to start.' The kid agrees."

What Andy Mayfair was paying for was protection; in the adult book-store business in New York, it's a necessity. Unless you are hooked up, someone from one of the Five Families is bound to butch in on your action.

"Okay, so now we got Mayfair paying us. I saw an opportunity in this and started to hit every adult bookstore in Nassau and Suffolk County I could find. What I'd do is go into these places, get to know the owners,

105

become friends with them and tell them, 'If you have any problems with anyone give me a call,' and I'd leave my cell number.

"Then I'd have a buddy of mine go in and say he was from one of the other Families—Genovese, Lucchese, made no difference. The guy would go in and say he wanted a piece of the action, smack 'em around a little. Then ninety-five percent of the time, I'd get a call from the owner to help him out. The reason most of these store owners would come to me instead of going to the police is the adult book business always involves some prostitution and various other things that law enforcement doesn't look too kindly upon. I'd get paid from the owners for arranging a sit-down where I handled everything."

Frankie pulled this scam twenty-seven times.

"Everything is goin' great. I've got twenty-seven stores and my route is growing weekly. That's the way I looked at it—like a cookie or bread route. So I'm collecting the money every week and kicking up to Tommy. Then, bang—this guy goes into Mayfair's place. This was real, not a set-up. And this guy was a Gambino trying to shake the kid down. So Tommy meets with the kid again.

"'I'm the guy to go to when you got a problem,' he tells Mayfair. 'I'm a capo in the Family.' I'd never heard guys do that, to say what he was. I was fucking amazed."

The surprises weren't over.

As 1999 wound down to a close, it looked like the Saggio marriage was doing the same.

Aria had just about had it. She was willing to accept that Frankie conned her initially when he didn't tell her that his businesses involved Mob shakedowns, shylocking, and extortion—to name a few. She wanted him to get out, which she considered a pretty rational request.

But Frankie hadn't. Further, with his reemergence in the Bonanno Family, he was deeper into the Mob than ever before. Frankie had told Aria all about his family's history; she felt that it was all "horseshit." There were no men left like his uncles. After numerous "discussions," they decided to separate.

Frankie took an apartment in the city that no one knew about. Or at least he hoped they didn't. He put the lease, the phone—everything under an assumed name. He owned nothing.

"I really couldn't anyway. My credit was blown from all the deals I'd done. I couldn't always use someone else's name. I also owed several million dollars to creditors and the IRS."

As the year wore down, so did Frankie. Feeling despondent, he went out to Spaghetti Park with Tough Tony from Parkside. They sat and ate their White Castles and watched the old men playing bocci. Tony commiserated with his friend about being part of Tommy's crew and once again told Frankie, "This life of ours is bullshit."

As New Year's Eve 1999 approached, Frankie could only hope that his future was a lot more promising than it looked. New Year's Eve that year was on a Thursday. For those working regular jobs, it meant a four-day weekend;: four days to party, recover, and get back to work. During that weekend, someplace on Long Island, Tommy D was planning a job.

JANUARY 4, 2000

"It was a usual Friday for me," Frankie remembers. "I got up in the morning and went for breakfast at the Frontier Diner on 3rd Avenue. After breakfast I went to buy a money order to send to Mikey Hollywood, who was serving twenty years in Sing Sing for armed robbery. Then I walked up to my office on 44th Street and Park Avenue where I was selling ATM routes at the time."

It is a measure of Frankie's fatalistic sense that he glossed over the fate of his best friend Mikey. Frankie knows no wiseguy, with the possible exception of his Uncle Jimmy, gets to live out his life quietly. You either go "inside," or you get your brains blown out.

What happened to Mikey Hollywood was that he had morphed into a criminal the newspapers described as "the Gentleman Bandit." Jewelry store owners described him as a polite, good-looking man in his early thirties. He would walk into their store, take a gun out from his attaché case and, politely, rob them of their goods.

Cops finally tumbled to his true identity and in 1997, Michael K. Groark was arrested as the Gentleman Bandit. Groark was eventually convicted of First Degree Robbery and sentenced to a minimum of nine years in jail. He is eligible for parole in May, 2007. Frankie made sure that he sent Groark money because he remembered how his so-called friends did not when he was in the Dannemora and the Nassau County lockup. More importantly, Mikey was loyal above all else, the kind of guy who was always watching your back.

"I missed Mikey. Anyway, I had gone to my office and while I was there, I got a call from Tony D.O.A., who is a soldier in the Columbo Family, to meet him at the cigar store on Mulberry Street at 6:00 P.M. We had held up two Columbians the week before and besides the 57K in cash, we took three kilos of cocaine from them. Tony took the stuff to sell. I never sold any drugs even though in our world, all Bonannos were tagged as dope dealers.

"At the time I'd had Mike the Moulie driving me around." "Moulie" is Italian slang for black man. "He met me in front of my office. We drove downtown to Mulberry and pulled in front of the cigar store.

"'Mike, wait in the car,' I said to him.

"Inside, behind the glass showcase, was a red door, I nodded hello to the kid, Joey, working the counter and went through the door, which read 'The Friends of the Castellammare Social Club. Members Only.'

"I was there as a kid with my Uncle Philly Lucky and it never changed. The bar is, like, red-button tuft with a picture of Mussolini behind it and there were several card tables, a blackjack shoe, and Joker Poker machines. It looked like a 1960s nightmare.

"'Hello,' I said to the guys playing cards and sat down next to Tony, who was drinking espresso and reading the paper.

"'I got 15K a key for a quick sale,' he says, really satisfied with himself, which I know means he got 18K. So we argue for a few minutes and instead of getting $22,500 I walk out with 26K. I said goodbye and went to Marilou's Restaurant to meet my friend Patsy for dinner and drinks.

"Marilou's is a wiseguy hangout in the Village on 12th Street. It's a dimly lit place with a long bar on the right side and tables on the left. There are two private dining rooms, one off to the left and straight back, another.

"Inside, Baron the coke dealer was sitting with Bruce Davis. Ever see those commercials for 'Call 1-800-Lawyers?' That was Bruce. Tito

Puente's brother was also there. I saw my friend Patsy, who already had an Absolut on the rocks with a twist of lemon waiting for me. We were gonna have a drink and then eat dinner. I had a lot on my mind.

"I was still trying to figure out what was up with Tommy D. He'd started going around to all the X-rated book stores—which is not normal practice for a capo—to go to the places we were extorting for protection every week. I really was worried.

"See, skippers never go to collect. The idea is to insulate themselves with guys between them and the mark. That way, in case a guy got pinched, he could honestly say his skipper had nothing to do with the operation. So at this point I am not sure if he is checking up on me or setting it up for me to suddenly become amongst the missing and he would still collect every week. This is worrying me. So I am gonna have a couple of drinks to loosen up.

"So we're hanging out at the bar, laughing and drinking, and decide to order some clams on the half and fried calamari. Bruce Davis sent us a drink, so we went over and said hello and started to bullshit. After awhile, Patsy said he gotta leave. I'm tired anyway and decided to go too. We walked through two sets of doors, up fifteen steps, and we were on the street."

And that's when Tommy D's crew tried to kill Frankie. Later, back at his apartment, Frankie stayed up all night waiting for them to come and finish the job.

"Tommy had known me since I was seven. He was an up-and-coming wiseguy and my Uncle Philly Lucky was his skipper. One Christmas my uncle made him come over dressed as Santa Claus and give presents to the kids. I'm sitting in the dark and remembering this and thinking 'I can't believe Santa Claus is trying to kill me.'"

The first smudges of morning light found Frankie still alive. He was determined to stay that way.

"I got out at dawn. I had my 9mm Glock in my waistband and 25mm five-shot in my ankle holster. I jumped in a cab and headed out to my mother-in-law's house on Long Island. John Giaccolone—he's with the FBI—he tracked me down there and he told me they already knew what had happened. That didn't surprise me. One way or another, those guys hear everything. They're as ruthless as we are.

"'Your life isn't worth a dime on the street,' Giaccolone told me. 'We've got you on tape extorting money from those adult bookstores.'

"You believe it? The kid who ran the adult bookstore, Andy Mayfair, was wired! He was working with the FBI. They got me on tape extorting payoffs and Tommy talking about his position.

"'We got you on tape with that American Paytel scam. We got you for mail fraud too,' the Fed told me."

But Giaccolone saved the best for last.

"'We're gonna arrest your mother, your wife, and your sister,' he says. 'We know they signed some checks for you in some of your businesses.'"

Which was true. Frankie had used his family's names in his businesses.

"'Sooner or later you're gonna disappear. You have no where else to go. We are the only ones that can protect you. Otherwise, you're dead,' Giaccolone said. What was I supposed to do? My Uncle Philly had always told me, 'Never be a stool pigeon.'"

Frankie remembered his first burglary and how proud his uncle had been of him when he didn't inform on his cousin Philip.

"What could I do?" Frankie repeats. "Go back out on the street and get murdered?"

Despite the fact that he was the Mob's biggest earner, in the end the money didn't count. Because he was not a made guy, the Commission didn't have to sign off on his murder. When he showed up dead, the bosses would just mourn the loss and justify his demise because Tommy D was a made guy and a capo. That's what made the whole thing perplexing; it was like tradition still applied, but at the wrong time.

Frankie had to deal with the reality. This wasn't a Hollywood movie. Frankie could be "among the missing" if he didn't watch himself. He was an outcast, a marked man. He was also confused, scared, and anxious. His stomach problems started then. He began taking over-the-counter antacids to cope with the heartburn.

Frankie didn't know where to turn. He needed help—somebody who understood the way the Mob worked, somebody in whom he could confide absolutely. He was separated from Aria but even if he wasn't, she only knew what he'd told her. She hadn't been born to the Mob like he had been.

• • •

The phone rang in the kitchen of Petrina Saggio's condo in Hallandale Florida. In 2000, she was a fifty-four-year-old woman who drank coffee by the gallon and smoked cigarettes incessantly—having a son in the Mob was stressful.

She perched the cigarette in the corner of her mouth and transferred the steaming mug of hot coffee into her left hand and picked up the phone with her right. It was Frankie.

"Ma, somebody tried to kill me."

"God forbid; I knew something was happening. You have to get out of there."

Frankie filled her in on everything that had happened, from the assassination attempt to the FBI's approaching him. He said he had to call her back, that he had to go. The line went dead. Frankie called again at midnight.

"What should I do?" he asked.

"Frankie, the FBI had to be looking at you before Tommy decided to clip you."

"What should I do?"

"Make a deal with the Feds."

"It's my honor—I can't do that."

"If you don't do that you'll be dead. They are not honorable men like they used to be. They are not like your uncle. They will kill you."

Life or honor? That was the decision Frankie had to make.

Frankie knew guys who had testified against the Mob. He knew what happened after that: they went into the Federal Witness Protection Program. It was just too much to think about. Frankie's head felt like it was going to explode; there was this incredible pounding in his chest, like he was going to have a heart attack. His stomach was on fire.

The pounding chest and burning stomach were nothing more than nerves. The only physical danger Frankie was in was from Tommy D. He knew that. Then he thought back to that day in 1981 when his uncle left for that final meeting and never came home—and was never found.

Frankie knew in his heart that the same thing was going to happen to him. His uncle used to say, "I'll never make fifty." If Frankie didn't watch it, he wouldn't either.

Philly Lucky's world had been a different one. Unlike Tommy, Philly Lucky took care of the men in his crew. They loved him. He didn't try to kill them. And if he had tried, he would have had the balls to do it himself.

"One night, Frankie was drinking. We were always very close and he's drinking and he starts crying, 'You're my sister, I'd never let anything happen to you,'" recalls Lina Saggio. "I didn't know if he was serious or messing around. I kind of knew what was going on but didn't know any of the details. I'm the baby in the family and they try to keep me out of it."

"Over the next few weeks, I kept seeing the unmarked cars going by over here," Lina says. "I didn't know if it was the cops or Tommy's crew."

Driven by self-pity, Frankie went on a three-day bender. When he sobered up, he started thinking rationally.

"I knew that in some way, as soon as I made my call to the Feds, the word'd get out on the street. But I wasn't worried about them getting me so fast. Wiseguys aren't world travelers. Take 'em off Mulberry Street and they don't know where they are. No, what I knew I had to do was stay away from any of my former hangouts. Especially clubs. That's where they'd find me."

They'd shoot him in the head and bury him whole in some lime pit that would slowly eat away at his body, or maybe they'd burn it beyond recognition and then dump it in the ocean. Or maybe they'd be more methodical: they'd carve him up and distribute him in pieces between New York, New Jersey, and—just to give his parts equal shrift—Connecticut.

Frankie and his mother arranged a plan. After they spoke, he got in the Dodge Durango and revved it up. He drove it down the West Side Highway and over the Washington Bridge. He got on I-95 going south and didn't breathe easily until the air outside began to turn warmer. As he drove further south, he stepped into summer.

"I got on a plane to New York," says Petrina Saggio. "When I got to Frankie's apartment, he was already out. I packed up all his stuff and called the movers. After that, I went to the airport."

When Frankie hit North Carolina, he started seeing the signs for

South of the Border. Those signs are probably the best friends of the drivers in the 1-95 southern corridor. They feature a Mexican-hatted gentleman named Pedro and witty sayings that end with a promise that you are only X miles from South of the Border. The signs appear frequently, teasing you with the sublime pleasures that can be found at Pedro's place. The signs provide the only intellectual stimulation on that mundane, boring highway.

By the time Frankie got to South of the Border he was tired and knew he could use some sleep. He figured it was as good a place as any and pulled in. South of the Border is actually an unwieldy conglomeration of souvenir stores, fast food restaurants, and a motel that seems, with all of its neon lights, like it would be more at home on the Vegas strip. It was a good, anonymous place to stay for the night.

Frankie paid in cash so there would be no trail for anyone to follow. After a restless night's sleep, he got back into the car for the homestretch to Florida. It actually didn't take all that long from South of the Border to get there—about two-and-a-half hours—but once he was in Florida, it was a whole other story.

The state is damn big! People always think of Texas and Alaska when they think of big states. Try driving to Florida from New York. It takes you almost all day to get from Florida's northeastern corner to the southeastern strip of Atlantic Ocean resort towns that have been turned into retirement communities by transplanted Easterners and Canadians.

It was evening by the time Frankie pulled into the parking lot in Hallandale. The sun was just setting and he looked up at the catwalks he had run on as a boy when his uncles were alive. He remembered screaming down to Scottie and how he couldn't figure out how an Italian guy had gotten that name. It all seemed like so long ago.

He trudged up the steps of the senior citizens' complex to the second floor and knocked on the fourth door down the catwalk. When it opened, he was looking into the smiling face of his aunt, Annette Giaccone, Philly Lucky's widow. Petrina Saggio had arranged it. They figured it would be the last place anyone would look for Frankie while the Feds worked out his protection.

Annette Giaccone had never remarried. She was still a beautiful woman with sparkling green eyes and a spine made out of cold steel. She got on the phone, dialed quickly, and said just two words into the receiver: "He's here." A few minutes later, Petrina Saggio walked in the door. She had flown ahead of her son. Their plan, so far, was working. Everyone laughed and hugged and then the women got down to business. Annette took Frankie into the back to show him the bedroom where he'd be staying.

Petrina took Frankie's car and put it in "somebody's" garage. When she got back to her own apartment, Petrina made supper like nothing had happened. And the phone rang again.

"It was someone calling with some kind of ruse trying to find me," says Frankie. "I'm sure they knew to look for me at my mother's. I hadn't told anyone where I was staying."

Ironically, it was even dangerous for him in his place of sanctuary. Philly Lucky's son, Philip Jr., the cousin Frankie had grown up with and thought of as a brother, was in Florida. Philip was still in the life. If he saw Frankie, he would have to make a call.

"Philip opened up a welding company down there. He's with the Genovese. How he got away with that move I'll never understand. He was never a fucking earner. He was a smart, big, tough kid and not a mover. Philip is two years younger than I am. He'd come to me and ask me questions."

Questions. That's exactly what Barney, the FBI agent assigned to Frankie's case, had started to ask him on the phone. Barney wasn't his real name; Frankie just called him that. It was the name of Rick Moranis's bumbling FBI agent, who relocated gangster Steve Martin in the Mob comedy, *My Blue Heaven*. Wiseguys thought Moranis was hilarious.

"I told Barney that I'd tell him what I could, but never, *never* would I talk about my family. Philip, anyone else—off limits. That was my only condition. They had to agree."

And they did. Philip Jr., of course, didn't know that and Frankie wasn't about to call and tell him. But if the two of them ever ran into each other, it could make for a very interesting afternoon.

WANTED AS THE ALLEGED VICTIM OF A KIDNAPPING

THE ABOVE PHOTOGRAPH IS ONE "JOSEPH BONANNO" MALE, WHITE, 59 YRS., WANTED AS THE ALLEGED VICTIM OF A KIDNAPPING.

AT APPROXIMATELY 12:20 A.M., OCTOBER 21, 1964, "JOSEPH BONANNO" OF 1847 EAST ELM STREET, TUCSON, ARIZONA, WHILE IN THE COMPANY OF HIS ATTORNEY, WAS REPORTED PHYSICALLY SEIZED IN FRONT OF 35 PARK AVENUE, MANHATTAN BY TWO (2) UNKNOWN WHITE MALES AND FORCED INTO AN AUTOMOBILE WHICH THEN SPED AWAY.

DESCRIPTION OF PERPETRATORS AS FOLLOWS:

#1 - MALE, WHITE, 6'2", 210 LBS., WEARING BLACK RAINCOAT, A DARK FEDORA, ARMED WITH A GUN.

#2 - MALE, WHITE, 6'0", 200 LBS., DARK CLOTHES.

GETAWAY VEHICLE WAS A BEIGE 2-DOOR SEDAN OF RECENT MODEL OF UNKNOWN MAKE, BEARING NEW YORK REGISTRATION PLATES.

ANY INFORMATION ON THE ABOVE, NOTIFY THE 13TH DETECTIVE SQUAD FORTHWITH: OREGON 4-0770 - OREGON 4-0771 - 777 3290.

Frankie's uncle Philly Lucky provided protection for Bonanno Family head Joe Bonanno at the Appalachin Crime Conference. Here is Bonanno at the time of his alleged disappearance in 1964. Credit: Library of Congress, LCUSZ62123538

Frankie's uncle Uncle Jimmy Clemenza bootlegged with Al Capone in Chicago during the 1920's. Credit: Library of Congress, LCUSZ62124511

Three men, Luciano, Siegel and Lansky, were the architects of the modern Mob. The most ambitious was Charles "Lucky" Luciano, photographed in 1935. Credit: Library of Congress, LCUSZ62114640

Benjamin "Bugsy" Siegel was a brilliant and violent man. His portrait was taken in 1935. Credit: Library of Congress, LCUSZ62-120865

Meyer Lansky, the financial brains of the Mob, photograhed in 1958. Credit: Library of Congress, LCUSZ62120718

Genovese Family head Vito Genovese, taken in 1959. Credit: Library of Congress, LCUSZ62123541.

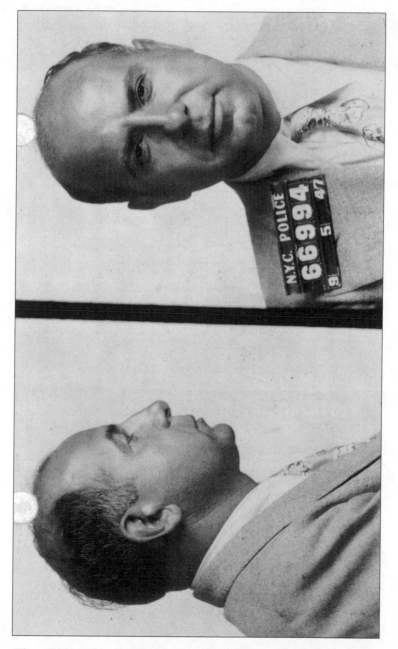

The affable and well dressed Carmine Galante, as caught for a NYC police mug shot in 1947. Credit: Library of Congress, LCUSZ62123540.

Chapter Eleven

CHEVY CORVETTE PACE CAR

Now that the Feds had their hooks into Frankie, they reeled him in.

"The Feds fly down to Florida and I met them at a hotel, where they took a room under a phony name. Inside, we had a little meeting. They had had a tap on Tommy's line. They play me a tape. It's Tommy talking to somebody on the phone in that code that wiseguys use on the phone. You know, you never use names.

"On the tape, Tommy calls me 'that crazy kid.' He tells somebody to take care of 'that crazy kid on Long Island—boom, boom, boom.' I knew it was me. And I knew what he was doing. He was ordering my death."

The Feds, though, had not played the tape just for the sake of assuaging Frankie's conscience about becoming an informer.

"I had to go back with them to New York. They wanted me to go meet with Tommy like nothing had happened. They were putting a case together for extortion and investigating several murders. See, they were trying to put a case together against him and I was their in."

They flew Frankie back to MacArthur Airport, a small airport in Suffolk County, Long Island, not far from Frankie's home in Islip where his wife Lisa still lived.

The Feds had yet another request of Frankie. "'Would it be out of line for you to ask Tommy for a gun?' Barney asked me.

"'No,' I answered, 'I'd asked him for one before when I was going to do something and I didn't have a gun.' Tommy was excited when he'd give me a gun because he knows I'm gonna go make money with it. And he'd knew I'd come back with cash, which I did on many occasions, so for me to ask him for a pistol would not be out of line. He always had a bunch of throwaways and he'd gimme one."

Frankie called Tommy and told him he needed a gun to "take down a dealer."

"'Come over now,' he says.

"So I go into Tommy's place, a cabinet-making shop that he owned, and I gotta make nice to him like nothing has happened and inside, my stomach was fuckin' twisted. I wanted to stick the fucking gun in his mouth but outside, I had to stay calm—and I did.

"'You got a dealer you're gonna take down?' he says to me.

"'Yeah,' I answered.

"'Come with me to the back room.' So we're in the back where he's got his office. He actually gave me a snub-nosed .357 Magnum. And then he says, 'Listen Frankie, this gun is bad because I think the barrel is bent on it. Whatever you're shooting at, it kind of goes to the left.' And he's checking it to see if it's loaded."

Tommy pulled back on the slide; a bullet was eased into the chamber for firing.

"And he gives it to me to go out and do the job. Now, you may be asking why didn't Tommy shoot me. Why not? Because he figures I'm gonna go out and make a quick forty or fifty thousand. Or more. And he gets his kick up. To him, it's worth it to wait another day or two until I bring him the money. He can do it any time he wants, but meanwhile he's makin' money from the stickup."

Frankie wore a wire for a few more conversations with Tommy. Each time, federal agents were stationed nearby. Finally, when Frankie felt Tommy's paranoia was heating up and he was getting ready to clip him for good, Frankie told the Feds no more.

Right before he was to go under their "protection," he was in a car in Huntington, Long Island, on Main Street. He had gone there with his former partners, Michael DeLucia and Robert Misseri, to have dinner at a wiseguy hangout called Maria's. The Feds didn't even know that their prize catch was there. He had gone on his own.

"'What, are you wearing a wire?' Robert asks me, and he puts a pistol to my head. 'It's over muthafucker.'

"'You better get that gun away from me before I make you fucking eat it,' I told him.

Robert looked at Frankie and saw that he meant what he said.

"'Just kidding,' Robert said, and he laughed. I laughed too, but inside I wanted to bust his fucking jaw. If it had been any other night, I would have been wearing the wire and I would have been dead. By the time the Feds got to me, I'd be stiff as a board.

"See, Robert figured I was OK; he was just fucking around. But he, like everyone else, was paranoid. The Feds kept grabbing everyone. That's why Tommy tried to clip me. He figured I'd flipped and made some deal with the Feds."

Of course, Frankie hadn't. It wasn't until Tommy tried to kill him that Frankie was actually forced to make the deal that Tommy feared. As for Robert, he too was so paranoid that he "even had a private investigator that worked for him," Frankie says. "The thing is, if he had been real about it, I wouldn't have let him search me unless I searched him too."

But it had been too close a call. Frankie Saggio had to disappear. Keyser Soze from the film *The Usual Suspects* could have taken lessons from Frankie on how to vanish into thin air.

It is hackneyed to say, but the wheels of justice do grind slowly. It takes time to prepare a detailed federal indictment, time to prepare a plea bargain agreement, time to arrange protection, and time to arrange a placement within the Federal Witness Security [formerly Protection] Program. While all of this was happening, Frankie started to move around. Like a real-life Richard Kimble, he hit the road as a fugitive and traveled from town to town under an assumed identity, all courtesy of the federal government.

For awhile in 2000, Frankie lived in Phoenix.

"Know what I hated the most about Phoenix besides the fucking heat? And if I hear one more person say, 'But it's *dry* heat,' I'll clip 'em. What I hated was that I couldn't get a good bagel there. I have to have a bagel every morning to start my day. With a shmear. Phoenix had lousy bagels, but their [base] ball team [the Diamondbacks] wasn't bad."

Frankie loves baseball, something he inherited from his father and his uncles. Brooklyn has always been a National League town, even though the Dodgers left almost fifty years ago. Guys like Frankie who grew up in the post-Dodgers Brooklyn of the 1960s and 1970s emerged as Mets fans who absolutely despised the Yankees. But over time, they had come to realize how much of a business baseball is, like everything else. Instead of rooting for a team now, Frankie rooted for professionalism. Baseball was one of the few things that gave Frankie a respite from his situation.

As the year wore on, his stomach got worse and worse. He started going to doctors and he was diagnosed with irritable bowel syndrome and acid reflux. The doctors put him on medication that alleviated the symptoms and the pain, but not the stress. Nothing could alleviate that.

From Phoenix, Frankie traveled out to California and checked into a hotel in Santa Monica. Every day while he was there, Frankie went walking on the esplanade that overlooks the Pacific Palisades. At night, he'd stand on the cliff smoking a cigarette, looking at the sunset down the Pacific Coast Highway. Seeing the green flashing lights in the distance, the snug homes overlooking the water, he felt strangely at peace and at ease, as if reality really was tropical breezes and palm trees. And then, just as soon as he was lulled, he would hear a strange sound behind him and suddenly turn.

But nobody would be there. Frankie knew his mind was playing tricks on him. He needed to calm down. Part of the problem was just the whole West Coast scene. There was no struggling there, not like at home. Everything seemed so easy; it was almost like it wasn't any fun—there was no challenge.

"I couldn't take it. I needed to get home," Frankie says. "I needed that New York edge. Once you got New York blood pumping through your veins, you can't live anywhere else."

Frankie really had no choice. The court had taken his passport; he couldn't leave the country. And he was wanted back in New York, in a federal Eastern District of New York courtroom. If the government wants to get a mobster to turn, it not only has to have something on him, it has to be willing to use it. That means filing an indictment, which is exactly what the Feds had done.

They didn't bother with the adult bookstores—that was simple extortion. Even elevated to a Racketeer Influenced and Corrupt Organizations Act (RICO) federal charge, it still meant Frankie could be out in a few years on parole. No, they needed to stick it to him hard and make sure he would follow through on any agreement he had with them for fear of being sent to Federal prison.

"United States District Court, Eastern District of New York," the indictment against Frankie Saggio began. It continued, "United States of America against Frank Saggio, Defendant. The United States Attorney General Charges," and then proceeded to list two counts against him, as follows:

```
THE UNITED STATES ATTORNEY CHARGES:
   At various times relevant to this information:


                     Count One
   1. The defendant FRANK SAGGIO directed and par-
ticipated in the day-to-day operations of American
Paytel, Inc. ("American Paytel"), a New York corpo-
ration located at 1111 Route 110, Suite 351,
Melville, New York.
   2. In [sic] or about and between January 1997 and
December 1997, both dates being approximate and
inclusive, within the Eastern District of New York
and elsewhere, the defendant FRANK SAGGIO, together
with others, knowingly and intentionally devised a
scheme and artifice to defraud American Paytel cus-
tomers and to obtain money and property from Amer-
ican Paytel customers by means of false and
fraudulent pretenses, representations and promises,
and for the purpose of executing such scheme and
artifice used or caused to be used the United States
mail.
   3. It was part of the scheme and artifice that
the defendant FRANK SAGGIO, together with others,
```

placed advertisements in publications, including "Pennysavers," that were delivered by United States mail. These advertisements solicited individuals to purchase payphones form American Paytel, as well as locations, known as "routes," from which these payphones could be operated and promised profits to individuals from the operation, when, as the defendant FRANK SAGGIO well knew and believed, he and other participants in the scheme did not intend to deliver payphones and routes to these individuals.

The indictment stretched another four paragraphs, detailing the American Paytel scam until it arrived at the second count.

Count Two

8. The defendant FRANK SAGGIO directed and participated in the day-to-day operations of New England Pay Telephone Corporation, Inc., which conducted business under the name United Pay Telephone, Inc. ("United") a New York corporation located at One EAB Plaza, Suite 165, Uniondale, New York.

Frankie had folded American Paytel when too many of his customers started complaining. He moved the entire operation a bit further west on Long Island to an absolutely gorgeous, glass-framed building on Hempstead Turnpike, a major east-west artery through the southern section of Long Island. The offices Frankie chose were plush and came complete with federal wiring.

9. In [sic] or about October 1997, the defendant FRANK SAGGIO opened and caused the opening of a corporate checking account in the name of United at a branch of the EAB Bank, a financial institution the

deposits of which were insured by the Federal
Deposit Insurance Corporation, located at One EAB
Plaza, Uniondale, New York (hereinafter referred to
as "the EAB account").

10. On or about and between January 21, 1998 and
January 26, 1998, both dates being approximate and
inclusive, within the Eastern District of New York
and elsewhere, the defendant FRANK SAGGIO did knowingly and intentionally execute and attempt to execute a scheme and artifice to defraud EAB and Key
Bank, another financial institution the deposits of
which were insured by the Federal Deposit Insurance
Corporation, located at 49 North Franklin Street,
Hempstead, New York."

Frankie had pulled in hundreds of thousands of dollars on the scam,
all in cash, that he had laundered through the EAB. That, of course, was
an additional violation of federal law. So far, the Feds had him on enough
counts of mail and bank fraud to put him away for life.

12. It was further part of the scheme and artifice that, on or about January 21, 1998, the defendant FRANK SAGGIO caused the deposit into the EAB
account of a personal check of a United customer,
in the amount of $10,000. This check, when initially
credited to the EAB account, created a balance of
approximately $11,339.92.

Now they were really going to nail him. The indictment continued:

The defendant FRANK SAGGIO deposited the check even
though (a) it was given by the United customer to
SAGGIO in exchange for payphones and routes, (b)
SAGGIO did not intend to deliver such payphones and
routes, and (c) SAGGIO was informed that a "stop

payment" order would be placed on the check if United did not immediately provide the payphones and routes that had been promised in exchange for payment.

•

The whole thing made Frankie's head spin. But that was the idea; it would move him forward and force him to make the deal—in writing. Frankie had no choice but to comply. He had his lawyer, Randy Chavis, hammer out the Cooperation Agreement.

A Cooperation Agreement with the federal government looks almost exactly like an indictment. For guys like Frankie who are pushed to the wall, it is no less than a lifeline. Frankie's Cooperation Agreement read:

1. The defendant will waive indictment and plead guilty to a two-count information to be filed in this district charging violations of 18 U.S.C. §1341 and 1344. The counts carries [sic] the following statutory penalties:

Count One

a. Maximum term of imprisonment: 5 years

b. Minimum term of imprisonment: 0 years

c. Maximum supervised release term: 3 years, to follow any term of imprisonment; if a condition of release is violated, the defendant may be sentenced to up to 2 years without credit for pre-release imprisonment or time previously served on post-release supervision

d. Maximum fine: $250,000 or twice the pecuniary gain, whichever is greater

e. Restitution: To be determined by the Court

Count Two

a. Maximum term of imprisonment: 30 years

b. Minimum term of imprisonment: 0 years

c. Maximum supervised release term: 5 years, to follow any term of imprisonment; if a condition of

release is violated, the defendant may be sentenced
up to 3 years without credit for pre-release imprisonment or time previously served on post-release
supervision
d. Maximum fine: $1,000,000 or twice the pecuniary
gain, whichever is greater.

As he read the numbers, Frankie's stomach rolled and he could feel the hot bile rising in his throat. The Feds had really thrown it at him: a total of thirty-five years in prison for his crimes. If he made parole in seventeen-and-a-half years, the mandatory time he would have to serve before he could even have a parole hearing, he'd be in his mid-fifties. Frankie looked through the agreement and thought about it and the promise he had made to his uncle so long ago that he was now about to break.

"You know something? The life is really what makes you turn. It encourages you to talk unless you want to wind up dead. It's not about honor or respect; it's all about making fucking money."

His stomach churning, Frankie turned to page nine of the agreement. Under the line "Agreed and consented to," in a bold, strong stroke, clear and unadorned, he signed his legal name: Frank Saggio.

There was nothing promised to Frankie, no reduced sentence. The Feds couldn't promise a *quid pro quo* because if Frankie were forced to testify, defense attorneys would use the deal to discredit him. Instead, there was an unwritten assumption that the Feds would provide a "word" to the sentencing judge. That "word" would probably result in Frankie getting no jail time. But Frankie's problems, of course, were far from over.

Frankie had been around the block too many times to expect that the Feds would be able to protect him from the Mob. Despite his obvious disdain for most of the guys he had done business with, Frankie knew that a smart guy like Robert Misseri could get him if he put his mind and his resources to it. Frankie believed he could be found no matter what the Feds did.

Had it not been for the threat that the Feds would indict his family,

Frankie would have just taken off. But he knew what he'd done over the past twenty years and knew the Feds meant business. He also knew that they needed him. And with his memory, if the Feds asked him the right questions, he could cripple the business activities of all Five Families and thus bring down the Mob.

As with all the other business deals he arranged, Frankie had a plan.

"Most of the wiseguys who go in [Witness Protection] don't think the government is very good at protection." Frankie agrees with that point of view. "I can do a lot better protecting myself than the Feds can."

He would enter the program, get his new identity, help the government build their cases against his former associates, testify if they wanted him to, and then he would disappear. He would depart Witness Protection and relocate in some place where the wiseguys would never find him. He had enough cash stashed away to start over somewhere else. Maybe he'd start a used car business or get into collision work. Who knew?

Frankie had been talking to Aria through all of the chaos. He told her about everything that was happening to him and started relying more and more on her for advice.

"I knew this was Frankie's chance," says Aria. "It was a chance to start over with a new name, a new identity, in a different place. I wanted to go with him."

Frankie and Aria reconciled. Frankie determined that once he was in the program, he would bring Aria in with him too. They would give her a new identity as his wife, and then they would disappear together. And live happily ever after.

Fantasy or Reality?

In J.K. Rowlings classic *Harry Potter* books, wizards and witches live in a separate, parallel world to the Muggles, the non-magical people. Frankie felt his world was much the same.

In Frankie's world there were wiseguys and civilians. The skills for existing in each world were not compatible. The man born to the Mob was now informing on it. He would forever more be on the run from the only family he had ever known.

Chapter Twelve

CHEVY CORVETTE CONVERTIBLE

"The Marshals Service provides 24-hour protection to all witnesses while they are in a 'threat' environment and upon their return to a danger area for pre-trial conferences, testimony at trials, or other court appearances."

—The United States Federal Marshals Service

New Yorkers call it "The Gap," and they don't mean the trendy clothing chain with the high prices.

The Gap is the Delaware Water Gap, a place where the Delaware River separates New Jersey from Pennsylvania, and it's easy to cross. Over the years, the area has become somewhat of a leisure spot with camp sites and various docks for launching boats onto the Delaware, which is gorgeous, placid, and stirring at the same time. Walled in with tall marsh oaks, pines, and cottonwoods, the natural beauty of the place is simply breathtaking. The government has set aside one long section of the area as a national preserve. For the less active tourist, there's a series of resorts set up by the Gap's waters. Caesars, the Pocomont, and other large resorts provide activities for both summer and winter. Of the latter, the Wildwood is one of the nicest. It's a place the government has also set aside for business.

The Wildwood Resort is located on Route 209 South near the national preserve. It was there that the federal government chose to put their star witness for the next set of federal prosecutions against the five Families.

Right from the beginning, Frankie's protection was lax. Aside from periodic physical checks to make sure he was safe, most of Frankie's communication with Barney consisted of calls to his cell phone. He had a room phone too, but it wasn't a secure line. The cell phone, they figured, was more private. Though he was under orders to stay in his room except to eat, Frankie couldn't take the boredom. No one could have, but Frankie was an earner: he was used to being active. So carrying his cell phone, he went out to make money in the wilds of rural Pennsylvania.

"I used to go there a lot with my wife—to Caesars—and I liked it. I liked Pennsylvania. I don't know what it was when I was there [under protection], but I found the place dreary."

Dreary or not, Frankie noticed that the real estate in the Poconos was steadily climbing in value. He bought the local paper and found out when the county had its monthly auction of local properties that had forfeited their mortgages. He went to the auction a week later and using his own money, bought some properties in his brother-in-law's name. He wanted access to them after his own name changed.

But the real estate was actually more of a needed distraction. On a regular basis he was questioned by the FBI, the United States Attorney's Office, and the U.S. Postal Service.

During those conversations, the Feds debriefed Frankie on the complete details of his criminal career: which Families he worked with, what crimes they perpetrated, the specific individuals he interacted with. If some agent was stupid enough to bring up his own family, Frankie would say, "No fucking way. That's not part of my agreement." He had been raised to keep his word and he would hold the federal government to theirs. Even on his side of the law, Frankie was a tough negotiator. And yet, like his uncle had taught him, he didn't win his arguments by dishonoring agents.

Just as the authorities had respected his uncle, the agents came to respect Frankie. They would vie for the opportunity to go to the Wildwood to question him, and not just because of his information. Frankie had been given a suite at the Wildwood. "It was actually a triplex, because above the second flood was a sleeping loft. I really didn't like sleeping in a loft that much."

Which makes sense because there were no lofts in Bensonhurst—or

Flatbush, for that matter. Only a trendy neighborhood like Brooklyn Heights or Park Slope had them. But what Frankie did have at the Wildwood and felt very comfortable with was a state-of-the-art kitchen. The agents began to deliberately schedule their debriefings so late in the day that it would be impossible for them to drive back to New York. They would use one of the suite's other bedrooms to sleep, but more importantly, Frankie would cook for them. All of the dishes that he had learned to cook over the years from his wife, his mother, his aunt, and, of course, the French-trained chefs at his restaurant, he now cooked for his new "friends."

"Those guys never ate so well in their lives," Frankie remembers. And Frankie spent months being questioned about a career in organized crime that spanned the late 1970s to the late 1990s. He fulfilled his end of his plea agreement. On April 11, 2000, Frankie picked up *Newsday* and got his first indication about how the information he was supplying was being used.

An article on page A3 in the main news section reported that the government had put together a RICO case, including murder charges, against five alleged members of organized crime.

Feds' Unusual List of Crimes/5 indicted in murder, arson, fraud scheme
by Chau Lam and Michael Rothfeld, Staff Writers

Their handiwork surfaced in a series of freakish and seemingly isolated incidents across Long Island over the past six years, federal prosecutors say.

First, it was found floating 30 miles off Fire Island in 1994, in the form of a gangster whose corpse had been stuffed into a 2-by-3-foot plastic tool trunk and set adrift at sea.

Then, in 1998, three men were arrested when an Old Brookville kennel went up in flames after fliers had been circulated complaining about barking dogs.

And in January, four others were charged with scamming more than 75 people by promising to sell them pay phones and phone routes through a company they called Bell Atlantic.

In an indictment that had even defense lawyers talking about "The Sopranos," federal prosecutors said yesterday that this all was the work of the Galasso Crew. They were, according to the indictment, a group of five men operating on Long Island under the protection of the Colombo and other organized crime families.

The men were indicted yesterday before U.S. District Court Judge Joanna Seybert in Uniondale, and a bail hearing was scheduled for Thursday at 4:30 P.M.

The five were: Saverio Galasso III, 33, of Woodbury, the group's alleged leader; Joseph Pistone, 31, of Huntington; Michael DeLucia, 40, of West Islip; Robert Misseri, 31, of Huntington; and Gary Hendrickson, 43, who pleaded guilty to arson in the kennel case and is serving a sentence in state prison.

Hendrickson and Pistone, who is in jail awaiting trial in the state arson case, were not in court yesterday. Galasso, Misseri and DeLucia pleaded not guilty and were held pending the bail hearing.

"I'll be fine; don't worry," DeLucia said yesterday to friends in court as he was led away. "This is a joke."

No Mike, it isn't, Frankie thought.

The five were indicted on federal racketeering charges that include accusations of murder, conspiracy, arson, mail fraud, wire fraud and money laundering.

Valerie Amsterdam, a lawyer for Galasso, said he is innocent. She said he had been about to leave for Disney World with his wife and four children because prosecutors said the indictment would be released Friday.

"In my opinion, the agents watched the final episode of 'The Sopranos' last night and decided it would be a whole lot better to bring the press out this morning," Amsterdam said.

Except this isn't The Sopranos, *this is real life*, thought Frankie.

She said Galasso invests in stocks for a living and said, "It's really sexy to make a case against someone whose name ends in a vowel."

Robert Sale, a Hempstead lawyer representing Misseri, said he is in the catering business.

Yeah right, thought Frankie, *and I'm fucking Prince Charles.*

"My client has no knowledge of this homicide," Sale said.

The murder charge involves the death of Louis P. Dorval, 30, of Nassau County, who authorities said was involved with the Lucchese crime family. His body was found by a charter fishing boat off Fire Island in August, 1994, the week after a federal indictment charged him and eight others in New Jersey as part of a ring of drugs, car theft and other crimes.

According to yesterday's indictment, Pistone, Misseri and a third, unidentified, person took Dorval in a car, where Pistone later shot him. Pistone and Misseri then allegedly put Dorval's body into a tool box. Pistone and the other person dumped it into the Atlantic south of Long Island, prosecutors said.

Frankie would later find out that Robert Misseri's private investigators were working overtime to find him.

The federal government's real goal in flipping Frankie was to get the Mob on stock fraud. The information Frankie gave them was the key element in building a case against the upper-echelon members of all Five Families for the stock fraud/brokerage scheme that Frankie had masterminded.

In an extraordinary series of indictments detailed in a statement dated June 14th 2000, the FBI released the results of Frankie Saggio's debriefings without ever once mentioning his name:

MARY JO WHITE, the United States Attorney for the Southern District of New York and BARRY W. MAWN, the

Assistant Director in Charge of the New York Office
of the Federal Bureau Of Investigation ("FBI"),
joined by RICHARD WALKER, Director of Enforcement
of the United States Securities and Exchange Commission ("SEC"), and MARY L. SHAPIRO, President of
NASD Regulation, announced today that 120 defendants, including members and associates of the five
Organized Crime Families of La Cosa Nostra in the
New York City area, have been charged with securities fraud and related crimes. Sixteen Indictments
and seven criminal Complaints unsealed today in Manhattan federal court allege fraud in connection with
the publicly traded securities of 19 companies and
the private placement of securities of 16 other companies. Included among the defendants are 10 alleged
members and associates of organized crime; a former
New York Police Department detective; 57 licensed
and unlicensed stock brokers; three recruiters of
corrupt brokers; 12 stock promoters; 30 officers,
directors or other "insiders" of the companies
issuing the securities involved in the frauds; two
accountants; an attorney; an investment adviser;
and a hedge fund manager. According to the charges,
21 broker-dealers or other financial adviser firms
were either involved in the frauds, or employed
stockbrokers or other persons who were involved in
the fraud. The various schemes resulted in total
losses of more than approximately $50 million, and
many tens of millions more would have resulted had
the schemes been completed. According to Ms. WHITE
and Mr. MAWN, this is the largest number of defendants ever arrested at one time on securities fraud-
related charges, and one of the largest number ever
arrested in a criminal case of any kind. In coordination with today's arrests, search warrants were

executed at four locations in New York, one in Dallas, Texas, and one in Salt Lake City, Utah.

Twenty-one defendants are charged with participating in a RICO Enterprise consisting of members and associates of the Bonanno and Colombo Organized Crime Families of La Cosa Nostra in the New York City area, that allegedly perpetrated massive securities fraud over a five-year period by forging corrupt alliances with members and associates of the remaining three New York City Organized Crime Families; controlling and infiltrating broker-dealers; conspiring with issuers of securities and individual stock brokers; scheming to defraud union pension plans; and employing tactics of violence, including threats, extortion, physical intimidation, and the solicitation of murder to further the illegal goals of the RICO Enterprise. The schemers used traditional boiler-room operations and current Internet techniques to carry out their alleged crimes.

The racketeering defendants include, among others: ROBERT A. LINO, a/k/a "Little Robert," an alleged capo in the Bonanno Crime Family; FRANK A. PERSICO, an alleged associate of the Colombo Crime Family, and a registered stock broker who controlled crews of brokers at various brokerage firms, including First Liberty Investment Group, Inc., William Scott & Company, Inc., and Bryn Mawr Investment Group; ANTHONY P. STROPOLI, an alleged soldier in the Colombo Crime Family who controlled crews of stock brokers; STEPHEN E. GARDELL, who is alleged to have corruptly exploited his positions as a New York City Police Department Detective and Treasurer of the Detectives' Endowment Association ("DEA"); GENE PHILLIPS, who controlled Basic Capital Management, the investment adviser to American Realty Trust, a New York Stock Exchange-listed real estate investment trust, or REIT; and WILLIAM P. STEPHENS, the Chief Investment Strategist of Husic Capital Management, a San Francisco-based investment adviser, who agreed to manage up to $300 million in union pension funds knowing that a portion would be invested in corrupt deals for the purpose of funding kickbacks to members of the RICO Enterprise and corrupt union officials. The RICO Enterprise is alleged to have engineered manipulation schemes in eight publicly traded securities and to have defrauded investors in connection with three private placements of securities, including one by Ranch*1 Inc., a company that operates fast food restaurants in the New York City area and elsewhere. Two officers of Ranch*1, SEBASTIAN RAMETTA and JAMES F. CHICKARA, have been named as defendants in the RICO charges and are alleged to be associates of the Colombo Crime Family.

In addition to the racketeering charges, the other Indictments and Complaints unsealed today charge a wide array of stock market schemes designed to fleece the investing public. Sales of stock in private placements are alleged to have been fraudulently rigged for the benefit of insiders and corrupt brokers. The Internet was allegedly used to further the schemes through the fraudulent promotion of stocks on Internet websites, or the use of companies that were touted as Internet or "dot.com" companies in order to induce investors to capitalize on the Internet boom.

Today's charges are the result of a highly successful, one-year undercover operation conducted by the FBI's New York Office, in coordination with the SEC and with assistance provided by NASD Regulation,

Inc. The undercover investigation involved, among
other things, surveillance, the use of undercover
purchases of securities, the use of a series of
cooperating witnesses who posed as willing participants in ongoing criminal schemes, and the instal-
lation of court-authorized eavesdropping devices in
the office of DMN Capital Investments, Inc. ("DMN
Capital"), a financial adviser firm that held itself
out as providing investment banking and stock promotion services.

The next day, June 15th, 2000, Frankie, a computer aficionado, logged onto premier Mob reporter Jerry Capeci's website, *www.gang-land.com*, and read his weekly column.

Doing What Comes Naturally
by Jerry Capeci

Six Gambino wiseguys, including a capo allegedly involved in the Paul Castellano rubout, and a Bonanno capo have been nabbed on extortion charges for separate shakedowns against the same smut peddler.

All the mobsters stood accused of extorting money from Andy May-fair's adult bookstore. As for the dispute between the Gambinos and the Bonannos over who had the right to extort the business, Capeci's column said, "I won the sit-down," the lone Bonanno defendant, capo Thomas Difiore reputedly told the store owner, "You don't pay nobody but me."

Tommy D was arrested at home by the FBI, who seized two guns, including a loaded .22. He was held without bail.

"When I was finished reading, I smiled and said a prayer: 'Rest in peace, Uncle Philly,'" Frankie recalls. No one knew that the indictment had been put together by the wire Frankie had worn for a brief time after the Feds flipped him. The idea was for Frankie to remain silent in the background, to continue to put together as many cases as possible, and only come out of the shadows to testify at trial if it were necessary.

The hope was that with the corroborating evidence the FBI had developed, most of the defendants would plea bargain and Frankie wouldn't have to testify. It was entirely possible that none of his former associates would ever know, for sure, that it was Frankie who put them away.

In February 2001, Frankie got a call at the Wildwood from one of the Secret Service agents in charge of the New York office.

"They wanted to talk to me about the counterfeit money order scheme I had going with Philip a few years back. I told them part of my agreement with the government was that I would not answer any questions concerning my cousin Philip or any other members of my family, but I'd answer any of their other questions."

The Secret Service agreed and Frankie found himself at 6 A.M. one morning, parked in the lot of one of the fleabag motels that line the shores of the New Jersey Palisades, directly across from the George Washington Bridge.

"There were three guys in a black 2000 Taurus that pulled up. I got into their car in the back seat with one of their guys on either side. The one in the front drove over the bridge, then down the West Side Highway. He went down the ramp onto West Street, by the piers, then all the way downtown. He turned in at Chambers, then up Broadway to the World Trade Center. He went into a garage in Building 1. We got out and then took the elevator up to their offices."

The Secret Service had offices at 1 World Trade Center.

"They took me into a conference room. They asked me what I wanted for breakfast. 'Get me an everything bagel with a shmear,' I said. After the food came, we sat for a few hours and they asked me all kinds of questions about the money order counterfeiting operation. I wouldn't tell them who my partner was because it was Philip. And I wouldn't tell them who had printed the stuff up for us. That guy was a civilian, legitimate. Why destroy his life? But I gave them some details about how the product was produced. One of the Secret Service agents said they were so authentic, they even contained the watermark.

"'Detail is my specialty,' I told the agent. When a money order or any kind of official bank check is held up to the light, there is a distinctive watermark that can be seen. I had gotten my printer friend to do that pretty good. Anyway, sometime in the afternoon, we were finished. They drove me back out to Jersey; I picked up my car and went back to the Wildwood."

By May 2001, the federal government was, to say the least, very satisfied with the information Frankie had given them. Using it, the U.S. Attorney had put together over one hundred indictments and literally thousands of charges against members of the Five Families. In a sense, it was Philly Lucky's revenge. But that revenge carried a heavy price for his nephew.

Skippers were trying to find out who the informant was. Sooner or later they would know for certain that Frankie was in the government's corner and they would come to get him. Strangely enough, the government, Frankie's lifetime foe, was his only ally. But he didn't trust them, either.

Frankie knew that he was worth more to the government alive than dead: he was a commodity. They could not only have him ready to testify, they could keep questioning him. And Frankie had an amazing memory not only for names and dates, but for details too. There wasn't anything he had done in his twenty years with the Mob that he couldn't recall.

Barney decided that things had gotten too hot. He discussed the situation with his boss at the Bureau and the decision was made. It was time for Frankie to go into the Federal Witness Security Program. It was time for Frankie Saggio to cease to exist. That decision coincided with Tommy D's trial.

MAY 26, 2001

The information Frankie gave the Feds helped them put together the cases against Tommy D and two Gambinos, capo Salvatore (Fat Sally) Scala and soldier Charles Carneglia for extorting the money from porn store owner Andy Mayfair. According to court papers, Scala was one of the assassins in the execution of Paul Castellano, the man John Gotti also killed to become boss of the Gambinos. Carneglia was involved in the retribution murder of a man who accidentally killed twelve-year-old Frank Gotti [John's son] in a 1980 car accident.

Frankie did not testify at their trial or Tommy D's; it wasn't necessary, the Feds felt, since they had an overwhelming case against the gangsters. But, you never know what a jury is going to do. Tommy D sat anxiously in his chair when the jury filed in with their verdict.

"Will the defendants please rise?" intoned the judge.

The three gangsters got to their feet. All were dressed nattily in suits and ties. The jury proceeded to acquit them of racketeering and extortion charges, which made Tommy hopeful. He really thought he was going to walk, until the jury came back on the third count: they found all three gangsters guilty of conspiracy to commit extortion. Tommy gasped audibly.

Newsday reported Tommy's fate this way:

> Thomas DiFiore, 57, of Dryden Way, Commack, a captain in the Bonanno organized-crime family, pleaded guilty Monday to [extortion] in federal District Court in Central Islip.

Rather than face trial again on this last count, all three pleaded guilty to conspiracy to extort. Tommy D was sentenced to three years in Federal prison. His expected release date is the first day of spring, March 21, 2004. When Frankie found out about the conviction, he didn't have time to breath the proverbial sigh of relief that, at least for a while, he didn't have to worry about Tommy.

Once again, the Feds were keeping him busy.

In the film *Eraser*, Arnold Schwarzenegger plays a federal Marshal who easily arranges for federal witness Vanessa Williams to disappear into a new identity. In one scene early in the film, Schwarzenegger's character uses a fancy computer program to fashion her a new identity in about fifteen minutes, including a credit card, a driver's license, and a social security card. The scene is pure fiction.

"That social security number is impossible to get; it cannot be forged. A new social is what really gives you your new identity," Frankie explains. "And that takes months to get, even after you go inside the program."

The Federal Marshals Service is populated by yuppified lawmen like Dwight Hubbard. Hubbard was a marshal who worked the Witness Security Program and he liked things orderly and neat, and he was definitely working in an organization that typified those values. Since 1970, more than 6,800 witnesses have entered the Witness Security Program (WITSEC) and have been protected, relocated, and provided with new identities by the Marshals Service. It is a record unsurpassed in law enforcement. The program itself is popularly referred to by the public as the Witness Protection Program.

Of course, that kind of success means there's a lot of these witnesses roaming around with assumed identities in the most benign of places. It comes as a shock when such a community learns that it has a fugitive living among its citizens. This program's work, which involves producing a new name, new social security card, new driver's license, and new credit card, is extremely painstaking in detail. The marshals aren't appreciative if, after all this work, a witness spits on them by splitting. When Frankie got the call from Dwight Hubbard, it was into this environment he was on the brink of entering.

"'You got to go in the program tomorrow,' Dwight says.

"'I'm not really ready,' I said to him. I was with my wife in New Jersey. Dwight didn't know she was there.

"'Listen, if you don't go in now, it will be another few months. Get your stuff together and we're going to come and get you tomorrow.'

"'Listen, all my stuff is up in Pennsylvania at the Wildwood.'

"'How about I meet you in Jersey, over the bridge?' He's, like, 'I got no authorization to pay for an overnight stay in Jersey at a hotel.' I ended up paying for his hotel room. I never got the money back."

Frankie was going to have to start watching his spending habits. During that last night in the Jersey hotel room, before he entered the Witness Security Program, Frankie and Aria made love. Aria got pregnant. Frankie was going to be a father for the second time.

Chapter Thirteen
GOVERNMENT CHAUFFEURS

The rendezvous took place at a prearranged point near the George Washington Bridge. "Dwight picks me up and he takes me into Manhattan, takes me to the Marshal's office downtown near the Foley Square courthouse," Frankie recounts. "They have this huge building there, all fortified and everything.

"Inside, they took my bags. You're allowed to bring a seaman's trunk and two carry bags. And then they take your trunk, put a padlock on it. They run you and all your stuff through the X-ray machine to see if you have any weapons, drugs, shit like that. And then they put you into a room with no windows, no doors, and no nothing. Just a little room where you can't hear; the walls are padded, the doors are padded, you can't hear anything. And they basically leave you in that room. They go outside and prepare whatever they have to, paperwork and all kinds of shit. They took my cell phone away. After awhile, Dwight came back in.

"'You are going to be transported to the airport by the Secret Service,' he said. 'Your flight leaves in about an hour.' Then they took me outside and put me into a blacked out Suburban, with three Secret Service guys: one driving, two in the back. We headed for La Guardia."

Considering the Feds were in a hurry, they probably took the fastest route to the airport from downtown: over the Brooklyn Bridge and a mere twenty minutes over the perennially rutted Brooklyn Queens Expressway to La Guardia Airport, an international airport within the borders of the city, in the borough of Queens. It's one of the busiest airports in the country.

"They get out first at the terminal. Then two guys come back and they walk me toward the curb.

"'Just walk like you're on your own.' So I do. They got guys in the airport. You can see them high signing guys as you're going through. You know, they got a guy on the pay phone sitting there and he's talking. They got a guy reading the newspaper, he's there. You know, you can see who's with them."

But only if you're a criminal or an agent. To the average person with an untrained eye, nothing special appears to be going on.

"And all of a sudden, some guy walks up to me and just hands me a ticket. As he's walking past me he says, 'Read the ticket so you know your name. Be the last person on, first person off at every stop.'"

Frankie looked up. He was in front of a 737 that was loading. He looked down, read the ticket, and saw that he was traveling under the name "John Bocabella."

"I walked right on the plane. They had already checked me in at the gate. Actually, I didn't know where I was going until I was on the plane. Turned out I was flying to Dulles."

In ninety minutes, the plane taxied from the La Guardia gate, took off, flew to an altitude of 21,000 feet, descended, and landed at Dulles Airport, Washington, D.C.

"I just walk off the plane and there is another guy. He hands me another ticket. He tells me the same thing: 'Last on, first off.' This time I was flying into Florida, Tampa/St. Pete Airport. I get out. The same thing happens. Guy walks over to me, gives me a ticket and tells me the same thing.

"'Last one on, first off,' he says, only this time he adds, 'A guy'll meet you in the airport.' So now I know it's gotta be the last flight of the day. This time I'm going to Virginia on a commuter flight."

Frankie's destination was Roanoke Airport, Roanoke, VA.

"A guy meets me in the airport. I don't even have to look for the guy, he just picks me right out. We were in rural Virginia. I think it was probably pretty easy for him to pick me out of a crowd. And he comes over, introduces himself, and shows me his credentials. Basically, he just tells me, 'OK, let's go.' He takes me to a hotel, makes me wait outside, goes in and registers me, gives me room keys, gives me, I think . . . well, in New York City they gave me five hundred in cash, traveling money. Then I get to Roanoke, I think the guy gives me another, maybe, fifteen hundred."

Everyone who goes into the Witness Security Program first has to check in at the top-secret base in Virginia, Frankie figured it must be nearby.

"I stay in the hotel a week, probably about two weeks until a spot opens up in the main building. The guy comes in my room one night and tells me I'm moving tomorrow."

The next day, Secret Service agents took him to Roanoke Airport.

"They flew me into Dulles again. A guy met me there with a bunch of agents and they had three Suburbans blacked out. It was a black Suburban with red interior. You can't see the driver and they have got Velcro felt over all the inside of it. So it's all, like, bulletproof glass. You can't see out. They take me on a forty-five-minute ride and the next time I get out I'm inside of some garage somewhere.

"I get out. Same deal: a bunch of agents take my bags, ask me if I have any drugs, weapons, anything like that. And they run my stuff through the X-ray machine. Next they take me up a long hallway. And all you can see in the hallway is the doors. Just a long, long hallway. It looked like a long hallway in an apartment building in Manhattan. All doors. And outside each door there is a keypad, like an alarm keypad. And he walked me through, takes me over to this room, punches in a code, and opens the door. He takes me in and it's basically a one-bedroom apartment."

Frankie looked around. The place was well furnished in that funky, cheap, chic decor, like the marshals had an account with IKEA. Frankie continued looking around.

"There is a back door with a very small—maybe ten-by-ten—cement porch. And there is a camera in the yard. You can go out in the yard. And there is a phone in the room.

"'Pick up the phone if you need anything,' Dwight tells me. They'll bring you whatever you want.' He gives me a list with all kinds of food on it.

"'Write how many of each thing you want on the list and I'll come back and pick it up in fifteen minutes.' So I go through the list, I write down what I want—it was all microwave stuff. I write down five cheeseburgers, ten boxes of cereal, milk, water. He comes back with a shopping cart like he went to the store and he's got all the stuff in it.

"'When you run low, pick up the phone and somebody will come and bring stuff to you.'"

Over the next seven days the marshals put Frankie through a series of tests.

"They give me all kinds of tests: IQ tests, personality tests, block tests, putting puzzles together—all kinds of shit like that. Basically, they give you to a psychiatrist and he gives you a bunch of tests, putting all these puzzles together, and he times you. Just to see if you're insane—I don't know—out of your mind."

Frankie wasn't.

"The psychiatrist told me, 'You have a very high IQ.' I think he said 138? It was above average. He said I was extremely advanced in math. I was at the level of math where you would get a degree for accountancy."

Frankie, though, never lost sight of the ball: he was there to get a new identity and then eventually split from the program.

"I'm still in the room and Dwight comes in and he says, 'Go to the phone book and pick a last name.' That's what I did. He says, 'I'll be back in twenty minutes.' He runs out of the room, comes back ten minutes later and says, 'This name is fine.' He comes back with social security paperwork, birth certificate, and all that shit.

"'You have to pick another last name for your mother, maiden name,' he tells me. I don't know, I guess it was for security.

"'Go ahead, you pick it,' I told him. He did. I said, 'Your choice is fine.' And that was it. Now they had to prepare my new driver's license, credit card, passport, and birth certificate.

"'It'll take around six weeks before we get everything to you,' he tells me."

Frankie would be moving before then. At the end of the seventh day, Dwight came to Frankie's apartment just as Frankie was in the middle of trying to make pasta primavera. He'd managed to get Dwight to buy him some fresh tomato sauce, cheese, vegetables, and a good, whole wheat pasta.

"'Get your stuff together, Frankie,' he says, 'You're moving tomorrow.'"

JULY 2001

"When I got to Virginia the first time the marshal, Dwight, took me to motor vehicle and got me a picture ID to carry around. He just basically walked in, told me to fill this paper out. He high-signed the guy at the counter; the guy just took the paper, took my picture, and gave me an ID. That was it.

"'It's going to be another day or two, and then we're going to take you up to your final destination,' Dwight said. Then he actually comes in at the end of that day and he gives me videotape of where I'm going. The place they'd picked out for me was Madison, Wisconsin."

The capital of "The Dairy State," Madison is also the home of the University of Wisconsin. It's a charming town with little bistros and coffee shops on the shores of the lake. "The videotape shows you restaurants, what the main industries are, hospitals; you know, how the economy is. And how many people live there, what the town is like. And all that shit. It's just like a video if you were going to move somewhere and they would show you what everything is like."

How did Frankie feel about the choice? "You can freeze your ass off there in the winter," he says.

Once again, Frankie was off. He followed the same routine: he was handed off from agent to agent, went from plane to plane, airport to airport, from Mobile to Memphis, Memphis to Chicago, Chicago to his final destination, his new home, Madison, WI—all in one day. Three agents picked him up in Madison and took him to the Marriott in town.

"Actually, I was at the Mariott there for about six weeks. Because I couldn't get a residence or anything like that until I got my new identity. That takes time. I needed a driver's license and a social security card.

"Well, they took me, actually, to motor vehicle and got me a new ID under the name—that new name—just an ID. And I had to wait for my social security number to come through for me to go get my driver's license. Finally, about a month after I get to Madison, I get the social security number.

"'We'll have to rent one of those car-teaching school places; you know, that teach you to drive—driving school. We'll have to rent one of those guys and let him bring you for the driving test,' Dwight says. But he doesn't do it, I do it. Because I don't feel like waiting and these guys ain't speedy. So I call up a car place, I put in the order.

"'I'm going for my driving test,' I tell the guy, 'I need you to pick me up.' I make out like it's my first time. He picks me up, I go, take the test, pass, of course, and I get my driving license.

"Now while this is going on, I get an allowance from the Feds for living expenses—eighteen hundred a month, a fucking joke. I used to spend that in a night on dinner and some drinks. Some of that I use, some I send back to Aria for house expenses. So I wait. I'm sitting in the hotel, bored out of my fucking mind, watching movies, walking around, working out, whatever shit I can think of to kill time. Finally my driver's license comes through and I'm ready to move out of the hotel.

"'Go out and find yourself an apartment,' Dwight tells me.

"I get a realtor to get me a nice two-bedroom apartment with a view of the lake. Nice place.

"'Go to the furniture store, pick out what you need,' says Dwight, and he gives me my allotment for furnishings. It was, like, fifteen grand I could spend on everything."

Frankie now had his new identity, his new apartment, and his new furnishings. It was time to check in with his federal parole officer, which was interesting considering he hadn't yet been convicted of any federal crime. So why the contact with a federal parole officer?

"What had happened was I was still on parole from that concealed weapon charge I'd served a year in the Suffolk County lockup for. Even in Witness Protection, you can still be on parole for a previous violation under your old identity. The parole follows you. So my parole, on a state charge, had been transferred to a federal parole officer who I had to check in with once a week."

Frankie checked in with a Federal Parole Officer in Madison. With that done, it was time to get a job.

"All those tests I took with the marshals, part of that was to evaluate me to see what kind of job I'd be good at.

"'Your tests were evaluated,' Dwight says, 'and it came back that you would be good at hotel management, accounting,' some other shit, sales. Now I'm still planning on signing out of the program, but I gotta play ball until I'm ready. What I basically did was, I went down and applied for a job at a car dealership. I was going to go and start selling at a car dealership."

But under his new identity, he had no employment history. There was a way around the problem, though it entailed breaking the rules. Individuals in Witness Security aren't supposed to call their spouses. But Frankie did.

"I never stopped calling my wife when I was inside the program. What I'd do is get one of those prepaid phone cards. Then I had my wife FedEx me a computer to the hotel under the name I was registered under. The marshals never knew. Then I would go online, and send her an email: 'Be at Uncle Sal's tonight at seven-thirty,' something like that, in case there was a tap on our home phone. Then I'd call her at Uncle Sal's.

"'Honey,' I told her, 'I'm going to put you down as my boss on my last job without telling any of them this shit.' And then I said, 'Just verify my job, verify my income, and verify how long I'm there.' I shouldn't have done that; I violated the rules. Anyway, I got the two jobs I applied for and I took the job at a Chrysler dealer. Those Midwestern guys couldn't sell a snow shovel in a blizzard."

Frankie was scheduled to start the job on a Monday. On the Friday before, "I had an appointment set up to go and see the U.S. Attorneys who were prosecuting the cases against Tommy, Robert, and the rest of them. They had to go through the Marshal Service to set up an appointment to have a meeting with me somewhere neutral—it couldn't be where I was. And they would be contacted, you know, the same day and be told on the way to the airport where I would fly into. And then they would fly to where we met, be picked up by marshals, and taken to a place—another place.

"In other words, after we got to our destination, we wouldn't stay in the same hotel or anything like that. I wasn't allowed to see them before or after the meeting. I wasn't allowed to tell them where I was staying. I wasn't allowed to speak about the weather, I wasn't allowed to speak about any sports teams. Those were the rules."

Where did the Feds pick for the meeting?

"So I meet with them and I stay with them for two days; we're in Alabama, a very remote section of Alabama. Matter-of-fact, they were even like, 'Holy shit, this is a fuckin' dump.' You know? They were like, 'They couldn't bring us somewhere else?'

"So the next day I leave, going back to Wisconsin, and I'm on four different flights, bouncing back and forth—boom, boom, boom—here to there to there to here, and finally I get to Wisconsin. The fucking guy is not even there to pick me up—the marshal. I take a fucking taxi from the airport back to my hotel. This is their security.

"I went back to my apartment. I was sitting down, I called my wife. I called from my cell phone, which they didn't even know I had because nobody checked. So I called my wife from the cell phone, told her I'm back and everything. And I was sitting on the couch watching TV, back from the airport maybe a half-hour or so. And on comes *The Sopranos*."

Frankie Saggio has some very definite opinions about the relationship between the movies and the Mob, starting with *The Sopranos*.

"It's pretty good. Some things are ridiculous, like in the first two seasons, Tony's nephew Christopher, he'd be arguing with made guys. You'd never do that because you'd get killed; you'd go through your guy. It all depends who you are. That was far-fetched.

"During the third season when Christopher became a made guy, I laughed my ass off watching it because it was so close to the real thing. You still gotta go through the same rigamarole, just like he did on the show."

And Tony?

"In real life, a crew boss wouldn't go to a psychiatrist because it shows weakness—they'll worry he'll roll over. I never heard of *anyone* going to a psychiatrist. Anyway, they all think they're sane but they are all fucking out of their minds. You never met so many nut jobs who think that they're sane.

"Another thing. The Jewish record executive who hangs with Tony and his crew; when he has problems with some black record executive who's trying to butch him, Tony backs him to the hilt. He says, 'It's your call how to handle it.' That's because the Jewish guy is a major earner. He definitely is a reality-based character, probably on a couple of guys.

"Jews have always been in the record business. You had some tough Jews back in the days of the fifties and sixties. But anybody in that business was always connected. The way it was looked at, Jews were the brains and the Italians were the muscle."

Frankie knows that is a false impression.

"There's Jewish gangsters. There's a lot of Jews who got just as much respect as a captain. Look at Bugsy Siegel, Meyer Lansky; they helped form the Mob and those guys were notorious, and you know what? Meyer Lansky was a stone-cold killer. He made an 'undisclosed' amount of money and never went to jail. He died in Hallandale a free man. Remember, just because they're Jewish doesn't mean they can't bust your head with a baseball bat. That's the same as stereotyping Italians as wearing nineteen gold chains, speaking in 'deeze, demz, and doze' and that they're all in the Mob.

"See, that guy on the Sopranos [creator and producer David Chase], when he gets it right it's because of Junior Sirico; all they had to do was look at Junior. Everyone in Bensonhurst knew him," says Frankie. "He went to my Uncle Jimmy's funeral."

Except outside of Bensonhurst, Junior Sirico is known as the actor Tony Sirico. As an actor, Tony Sirico got his big break when he was cast as "Paulie Walnuts" in *The Sopranos*. The show was hailed as a critical success due in no small part to Sirico's dead-on portrayal of Tony Soprano's good right hand, Paulie Walnuts. Other criticism of the show pointed out its accuracy in portraying Mob life. Critics wondered who producer David Chase's secret source was for details.

"It's Junior," says Frankie.

Actually, it's Genaro. New York State court records show that Genaro Sirico, a.k.a. Tony Sirico, was convicted of felony weapons possession in 1971. The indictment against him includes other felony charges. He was sentenced to four years and served twenty months in NYS prisons.

"Junior's always been connected to the Columbo Family, through my cousin Jimmy Brown Jr. It's understandable how close they [*The Sopranos*] were and how on-target they were. The reason being, of course, you live in NY and NJ, you know about gangsters.

"I remember Joe Pesci. Joe Pesci's best friend was a captain in the Genovese Family, named Joe Dente, Sr. Dente went out to L.A. and got into the movie business. So where does Junior get his character from? From growing up around it. How does Martin Scorsese make the films he makes? He grew up on the Lower East Side in Little Italy. How does he know how to make characters walk and talk like wiseguys? Because he lived on the same block as the real guys. He grew up around it. These guys don't just come up with such an on-target adaptation of how to act as a wiseguy by reading books. They lived with them; they were friends with their sons and the sons' kids. How did I pick up certain mannerisms? How do you know how to answer someone? You learn what you see."

But more often that not, the TV image of the Mob is flawed.

"*Falcone*, that show on CBS with Jason Gedrick and that guy with the bushy eyebrows—that was a fucking joke. I love *The Godfather* movies except the third one where the woman took over the crew—that was a joke. That ruined the whole saga."

The woman he's referring to in the film is Michael's Corleone's sister, Connie Corleone, who does literally run a crew in the film.

"When Francis Ford Coppola threw her in as a boss, that was a joke. I don't know why he did that."

Frankie was not aware that Talia Shire, the actress who played Connie is Coppola's sister. Coppola compromised the reality of his story to give his sister a juicier part.

"*Godfather III* went off on a wild goose chase. I mean, George Hamilton as a consigliere? You know, after Sonny Franzese's son got out of the Witness Security Program, he went out to Hollywood and went into the movie business. I think every fucking gangster wants to be a fucking movie star in their heart. It's just a production. Like in the joint: everybody likes fucking attention. They say you're supposed to have anonymity, but today everybody wants people to know who they are. My uncle never believed in that. It was his business; he kept it private. It was a secret society and that's the way it should have stayed. If he was around today, he wouldn't agree with any of this crap.

"My uncles were in the life for the money, not the fame. These guys today, they want both, which only makes you end, up in jail, just like John Gotti—and look where he wound up. His whole fucking family is in jail. My uncles, they were tough guys, not phony gangsters. My Uncle Philly was quiet and reserved. Uncle Jimmy was just the opposite—very loud. He'd tell you whatever was on his mind. He didn't give a fuck; he was a very feared guy. They would not want a guy to bring unwanted attention to their business because it makes it that much more difficult to *do* business.

"My Uncle Philly would get a traffic ticket and pay it the same afternoon. Today's gangsters, half of them like the attention. I know one shylock who was calling the news on himself so they'd cover him collecting.

"Listen to this. There's this Tony Damonte who killed a DEA agent on Staten Island. I knew him; he was a maniac. The fucking cops and FBI made it impossible to do business after that. They wanted Tony. Instead of making the kid turn himself in, they killed him out in the street so the police found him. They wanted the cops to stop fucking with everybody's business."

Even if Tony Soprano is shot in the last episode of the series, James Gandolfini, the actor who plays him, gets to walk away after the last take. Not so in real life where in the last reel, you might not walk at all.

"So *The Sopranos* was over and I started getting chest pains—really bad chest pains. And I said to myself, 'Maybe it's heartburn or something.' So I go out to the little dairy, gas station—whatever the hell it is, Speedy Mart—and I get a Diet Coke, figured maybe it's just gas. And I'm walking back—I couldn't stand still. I had to walk; I had to walk around because it was fairly a lot of pain. So I had the cell phone with me and I said, 'Shit, the pain is intense.'

"I probably could have made it back to my apartment but my address was so weird. I didn't want to go up to my apartment, have a heart attack and pass out, and then there ain't nobody going to find me, until someone reports a strange odor coming from apartment 3-A. So I walk out to the corner of Yellowstone Boulevard in downtown Madison. I use my cell to call an ambulance. The ambulance comes. They start giving me Nitro in the ambulance, oxygen, put an IV in my arm, and take me to the hospital.

"'I'm a resident,' the doctor tells me at the hospital, the first guy that sees me. 'You probably just got acid reflux and we'll keep you for a few hours and then you can go home.' About twenty minutes later, a cardiac specialist comes in.

"'Listen, you had a major heart attack. We're bringing you upstairs right now. You have some clogged arteries. We're going to go in and we're going to clear out that artery and put some stents in.'"

Stents are small pieces of tubing that are placed inside an artery to keep it open.

"They rolled me upstairs and at that point I told the lady, 'Just give me a phone,' and I called my wife, told my wife what happened, and she flew in the next day. I also called Barney and told him, 'I'm in the hospital, there is no need to come here. I had a heart attack.' The marshals would never let me tell him where I was. Any contact I have with them [the Feds] is through the Marshals Service."

By that time, Frankie had violated the basic tenet of Witness Security: he had told people where he was—first his wife, then his mother. The marshals wouldn't be happy.

The marshals jumped through a lot of hoops to get witnesses new identities and it infuriated them when Mob idiots like Sammy "the Bull" Gravano and Henry Hill threw it to the wind. But Frankie really had had no choice. He needed next of kin he trusted to make medical decisions should he become incapacitated.

"What was I supposed to do? Rely on Dwight or Barney to make those decisions for me? No fucking way," he says.

The stress of the past year had caught up with Frankie. That, a genetic predisposition to heart problems, and a thirty-year diet of fatty foods like his bagels with shmears. His echocardiogram showed that he had only one clogged artery: he was lucky. The angioplasty and the stent did the trick of opening it up. Frankie called Marshal Dwight Hubbard and told him he was going to be released the next day. That night, Frankie figures that Hubbard "called the nurses' station and the nurses' station probably told him, 'His family is here and he's resting comfortably. He's being released tomorrow.'

"When tomorrow comes, Dwight is actually in front of my apartment He looks up at my apartment—remember, it's all glass overlooking the lake—and he sees people in the window. Two women: my mother and my wife."

They had both flown in using their maiden names and they both had drivers licenses in those names, making it difficult for anyone to track them. Frankie was just getting dressed into his civilian clothes at the hospital, ready to be released, when the room phone rang. It was Dwight.

"'I'm outside your apartment Frankie.' Boom, boom, boom. 'Who is in your apartment?'

"'Listen Dwight,' I said, and before I could get started he gave me all this shit about how I violated the program, how it could cost me. All this shit. So I told him, 'I had a heart attack, and nobody even contacted my family? I called my family and they came down.'

"'Well, then that's a violation. I can't protect you now that people know where you are,' boom, boom, boom, and this and that.

"'Well,' I said, 'my wife and my mother flew in under their maiden names; they both had their license under their maiden names still.' Whatever.

"'You want to sign out of the program?' he asks me.

"I said, 'No, I ain't signing out. You throw me out.' He wanted me to sign papers to let them off the hook. So I wouldn't do it.

"'OK,' he finally says, 'I got to write a report. So, OK, I'll bring the paperwork and we'll sign you out.'

"I said, 'I'm not signing out.'

"He said, 'Well then I have to write a report.'

"I said, 'Well then write a report. You'll have to throw me out, I'm not signing out.'

"So it takes about another month. Now I'm getting banged; I'm getting sent hospital bills for ridiculous amounts of money. I think the total bill was, like, a hundred and seventy-five thousand or whatever. So now they have to pay these bills. Because he had screwed up and not put in my medical insurance paperwork to begin with. So I'm getting all these hospital bills and shit and they're paying them as they're getting them. And I'm still getting them today; I still get bills."

As for kicking Frankie out of the program, eventually the marshals realized that he probably had been right to call his family during a life-threatening illness.

"Now Dwight comes to me and says, 'Listen, we want to relocate you to a new place and keep you in the program.' They didn't want to let me out. In other words, Dwight had to go to his people in Washington and Washington said, 'No, he's staying, relocate him. We don't want to let him out. We're not going to throw him out, we just want to relocate him to another place.'

"I didn't want any part of that shit. I was sick at the time and I wanted to choose where I wanted to live. I had already gotten what I wanted out of them: my new identity. And at that point I wasn't going to be relocated, just bounced around for three months while they took care of all that shit."

In other words, Frankie was doing what every heart attack patient is supposed to: he was modifying his life and taking positive steps to reduce daily stress. He needed a place to rest and recover. Florida would have been great, but it was too "hot."

"A few weeks before this, I had called my Aunt Annette. She told me she had been in New York for an affair.

"'Frankie,' she says, 'I was at the buffet when Tommy D came up to me. He said, 'You know where Frankie is? I need to talk with him.' I said to myself, 'You know what? My husband was absolutely right for chasing him out.' He's got a lot of nerve and even if I did know—which I don't— I certainly wouldn't tell him or anyone else.'"

But if not Florida, where could Frankie go to recover? Frankie's sister lived in Georgia. She and her husband Kelly had a large house in a suburban neighborhood. The mortgage and deed were under names that no one would ever think of when looking for any of the Saggios.

Frankie called Dwight and told him he was signing out of the program and where he would be. He did the same with Barney and his federal parole officer. There were all kinds of forms he had to sign because he was dealing with the federal bureaucracy. When he thought he had signed all of them, Frankie flew from Madison to Atlanta. His sister, her husband, and Frankie's nephew, his godchild, met him at the airport. They drove Frankie to their home and for the first time in over a year, Frankie got to spend time—openly and legally—with his family.

AUGUST 2, 2002

Under the headline "Huntington Man Pleads Guilty," the article reported that "A Huntington man initially charged with taking part in an organized-crime murder that [was known] as 'the body in the box' case, pleaded guilty to money-laundering as part of a plea bargain reached in Central Islip yesterday."

The "Huntington man" was Robert Misseri. What the article didn't say was that Frankie had provided the government with enough information on their pay phone scam that the case against Misseri was overwhelming. On the other hand, Frankie's charge that Michael was involved in the "Cooler Boy" murder could not be made with any other evidence and so, the government had decided to deal.

Misseri plead to laundering $107,000 from the pay telephone scam in return for the government dropping the murder charge. With sentencing pending, Misseri was facing up to fifty-seven months in prison. That put Frankie's mind at ease. He figured he wouldn't have to worry any more about Misseri coming after him.

"So I'm recovering, beginning to feel pretty good. I meet with the Feds who come down from New York. Then I get a call from the marshal in Wisconsin—not Barney, my regular guy, but some schmuck.

"'Where are you?' he asks me.

"'Georgia,' I answer.

"'Where in Georgia?'

"'Abderdeen County. Near Marietta.'

"'OK, I want you to meet me to sign some papers. Meet me in front of the federal courthouse in Marietta.'

"So I go over there, my sister, and me. I meet the marshal on the steps of the federal courthouse. He has an envelope. In it are supposed to be yet some more papers to sign to get me out of the program. He motions to the envelope.

"'With me I have a warrant for your arrest,' he says.

"'What?' I screamed. 'Are you fucking kidding?!' I couldn't believe this. Muthafucker! I had just got off the phone with the federal prosecutor for the Eastern District of New York; we were going over my testimony.

"'They violated you for signing out of the program,' the guy says. 'You violated your federal parole by not signing all the right forms.'

"'Violated me?' I still couldn't believe it.

"'It's not my fault if you left,' the guy says."

It was a settlement of a business debt. Frankie had gotten his new identity—the marshals had seen to that. But he had made them look bad; he had left their program because of his illness. He figured he could protect himself just as well as they could. Which made the Federal Marshals Service look bad in front of the Federal Prosecutors' Office.

The marshals had become sick and tired of doing a lot of hard work only to have Mob guys just do as they pleased. And the federal attorneys? They didn't really care what happened to their witnesses so long as they showed up and testified. After that, who cared what happened to them?

And so Frankie Saggio was violated because, allegedly, he hadn't filed the proper forms to get out of the Witness Security Program, even though the real reason was that one branch of the federal government was flexing its muscles in front of the other.

"They took me to the federal building in Aberdeen County and they're processing me. Mug shot, prints—the whole thing. They make sure it's under my old name, not my new one. If they violate me under my new name, which they technically should because it's the name I'm using, then they have to start over with me. Instead, they violate me as Frankie Saggio."

For holding, the marshals put Frankie in the county lockup, which wasn't such a good idea. If a good reporter looks at the arrest sheets, they see the name of a guy specifically identified as a *federal* criminal. Plus, the jail was awful.

"They stuck me in with murderers, rapists, pedophiles—the scum of the earth," says Frankie. "The county lockup didn't segregate prisoners on the basis of offenses. I slept on a mat on the floor with these scumbags."

Not only was it a bad place for a man recovering from a heart attack, it was a bad place for the most important active witness in the Federal Witness Security Program.

A few hours later in Washington, Barney's phone rang.

"You have a collect call from an inmate in a correctional facility," said a tape-recorded voice. "At the tone, please says your name."

The tone sounded.

"Frankie."

"I'll accept the charges," said Barney.

"'Frankie, where the hell are you?' Barney asked me.

"'I'm in fucking jail. Your pals in the Marshals Service violated me.'

"'Violated you?'

"'Yeah. I didn't sign all the papers I was supposed to when I left Witness Protection. They say that violates my probation. They stuck me in the county jail with these scumbags.'

"'Look Frankie, this shouldn't be. I'll fly down tomorrow and get you out. But don't be an asshole and give these guys any trouble. It's a political thing. Like I said, I'll fly down and get you out.'

"I said, 'Okay, I'll be waiting for you.'"

The date was September 10, 2001.

Chapter Fourteen

LINCOLN TOWNE CAR

SEPTEMBER 11, 2001

"Ordinarily when Frankie was inside, I could do stuff to help him," says Aria. "I knew the right people to talk to: the lawyers, the bail bondsmen. I knew the right buttons to press, legally, to get him out on bail as quickly as possible. But this time I couldn't help him.

"I was five months pregnant and something had gone wrong. The ultrasound showed that the baby, a boy, was alright, but I would have to stay off my feet for the remainder of the pregnancy. I'd had two miscarriages before and I didn't want that to happen again."

Aria had gone into NBC and told them she was taking family leave immediately.

"I was flat on my back at home when Frankie called on the tenth to see about getting him out. I couldn't get down there; I had to look after the baby and myself. I was torn, but I knew that I was doing the right thing."

So did Frankie. He wanted to be with Aria but he couldn't leave Aberdeen County. Even if he got out on bail, his parole officer would violate him if he left. This time, there would be no getting out; they'd keep him inside until after he testified.

"The jail they had me in was a real shithole," says Frankie. "It was probably a hundred years old. It was dirty, damp, disgusting. Inmates were not allowed magazines, newspapers, or books. All they could do was watch TV. In a county lockup like Aberdeen's, there's a day room where guys crowd around a TV set on a platform above the floor so everyone can see. Guys pull up chairs and just watch."

On September 11, Frankie was among those millions of Americans who watched, live, as the planes piloted by terrorists crashed into the twin towers of the World Trade Center.

"I couldn't remember which floor I was in at One World Trade. But I knew that a lot of Secret Service agents got killed because they have an office right in there. It was the same place I had been in. I didn't feel too good about myself right then."

Frankie turned away from the surreal images. He had problems of his own; he needed to get out. He wasn't getting his heart medication. The guards were not giving it to him. Without it, he was in danger of having another coronary.

A few hours later in Washington, D.C., Barney's phone rang.

"You have a collect call from an inmate in a correctional facility," said a tape-recorded voice. "At the tone, please say your name."

The tone sounded.

"Frankie."

"I'll accept the charges," said Barney. He had heard from the marshals about Frankie's alleged violation.

"Barney says, 'I'm real sorry Frankie, I can't get you out right now.' What the fuck was this?

"'Listen Frankie, all the airports are closed because of the attacks—all over the country. I won't be able to get to you until they let planes fly again,' he said.

"'When's that?' I asked him. He didn't know. He said to just keep checking in with him everyday and to hang in there. Yeah, hang in there. He wasn't the one eating shit for food and sleeping on a mat on a damp floor. If it hadn't been for my heart, I wouldn't have cared that much. I mean, I knew he was busy doing whatever it is the FBI was doing to go after those muthafuckers who took out the WTC."

But Frankie was in danger, too, inwardly and outwardly.

Over the next few days, his physical condition worsened. He got a cold that developed into bronchitis. It wasn't until he'd been inside for a week that the guards finally gave him his proper medication. On TV, he saw that planes were flying again. One more time he called Barney. One more time Barney said he was working on getting him out.

"He couldn't explain exactly what the problem was, but I knew it was just the bureaucracy taking forever to process all the right forms, call the right person, all that crap."

Finally, two weeks after the World Trade Center collapsed, Barney flew down to Georgia and got Frankie out. For the next three weeks, into October 2001, it looked like Frankie Saggio would get a respite. He found a good cardiologist in Marietta, where he registered under his new name. The doctor adjusted his medication and gradually, he began to feel more like his old self. He even started working out again, which he loved. Then Aria called.

"My water had broken. They rushed me to Winthrop Hospital in Islip. I was only twenty-four weeks pregnant," Aria recalls.

Neonatal care has come a long way in the past decade. If the doctors could postpone her delivery until she was twenty-six weeks, the baby would have an eighty to ninety percent survival rate. At twenty-four weeks, the baby had only a fifty percent chance of surviving.

Aria felt the IV going into her arm, pumping her full with what she hoped were miracle drugs. For the time being, the medication worked: her contractions stopped. She was taken to a private room where the medical staff continued to observe her carefully.

"I wanted to drive up or fly up—I didn't care which," says Frankie. "I was all set to do it, but my family talked me out of it. Aria, too."

"Oh, I wanted him with me," says Aria, "but I knew they'd violate him again if he just hopped in the car and came."

There really was no sense in Frankie going to be with Aria; there was nothing he could physically do to help her. The Saggios settled down to wait, to see if the doctors could save their baby's life. That night, for the first time in years, Frankie went to church and lit a candle for his wife and their unborn baby.

On October 17, 2001, Aria Saggio gave birth to a twenty-six-and-a-half-week premie. The baby was small, but perfect: no birth defects, but his lungs were underdeveloped. He went on oxygen immediately. The child, the doctors said, would survive if everything went well. This time, Frankie did the right thing.

"I called my probation guy and told him what had happened, that I had to leave, that my wife had given birth prematurely. He said, 'OK, I'll find a guy in New York to handle your case.'"

More importantly, Frankie had to call Marshal Dwight and tell him what was up.

Dwight Hubbard offered a grave warning. "'You're going into the danger zone and the U.S. government cannot be responsible for your safety or the safety of your family,' Dwight said. Tommy D, every wannabe wiseguy, low-life piece of shit lookin' to make a name for himself was lookin' for me.

"'OK,' I said and just took off in my car. I made New York in about ten hours."

On the drive, Aria called Frankie to tell him that she'd been discharged. The baby, of course, remained in the neonatal unit and would be there for some time. When Frankie hit New York, it took him awhile to get through the checkpoints at the Goethals Bridge—the bridge that connects Staten Island to New Jersey—and the Verrazano Bridge, the bridge that spans the Narrows into Brooklyn. The authorities were still edgy, expecting another terrorist attack. Like other motorists, Frankie had to answer a few questions before they let him go through both tolls. Once he hit Brooklyn, it was only an hour out to the Island. But he arrived late at night, past visiting hours at the hospital.

Frankie parked down the block from his house. He looked first, to make sure no one was shadowing the place. When he was certain it was safe, he walked quickly up the walk and in through the front door. He and Aria embraced. With the lights dim inside the spacious colonial, they talked about the past few months. After awhile Aria grew weary and turned in, but Frankie was too keyed up to sleep. He poured a glass of Ambassador sixteen-year-old Scotch and sat down at the dining room table. He turned the light out. It was just him in the darkness with his drink and conscience.

It had all caught up with him: all of the grief he had caused people over the years, the people he had lied to and cheated, beaten, and extorted—it all came back to haunt him. He hadn't gotten away clean; the sins of the father were being visited on the son. And the wife.

How many more can things go wrong? he asked himself. *How much more suffering do we have to go through before it's over?*

The next morning, Aria drove to the hospital and they took the elevator up to the neonatal unit and followed the standard procedure to visit their son. The biggest danger to premature babies with immature immune systems is communicable infection. That's why Frankie, Aria, and everyone else on the unit first scrubbed at a hospital sink like they were entering surgery. After that, they turned the handles of the water faucets off with their elbows and put on light, sterile gloves. A snow-white gown and a sterile mask completed the outfit. Then Frankie and Aria followed the nurse through the unit.

Babies in all physical conditions were in the clear plastic bassinets and incubators that ringed the room. Frankie's son was in one of those incubators. He looked down at the boy, his little face scrunched up, his tiny arms as thin as the barrel of a ballpoint pen, the premature newborn skin punctured by an IV line through which flowed medicine and fluids. The baby had an oxygen clip under his nostrils, a feeding tube down his throat to his stomach, and on his chest, a sensor that monitored his heart rate. An EEC performed when he was born and on the previous day had shown his brain activity to be normal.

"I couldn't even touch him," says Frankie. "But I really felt, I don't know, just happy when I saw him. It had been a long time since I was happy about anything."

They named the boy Frankie Jr.

"I figured, why not do it?" says Aria.

At that moment, Frankie Saggio received the biggest gesture of love he had ever known. His wife wouldn't have named the baby after him if she expected him to die—from his heart or anything else. It showed not only that she loved him, but that she was confident things were going to work out.

Every day Frankie and Aria would arrive at the hospital early, before 9 A.M., and stay until well past 9 P.M. the same evening, just sitting by the baby's side, talking to him through the plastic bassinet, letting him know that his parents were there loving him. They placed a picture of themselves inside the bassinet, pasted up at the side, so Frankie Jr. could see his parents anytime he wanted.

Frankie remembers all too well what happened on the fifth day. "Me and my wife were leaving and I started getting chest pains.

"'No, not again,' I thought.

"So I told her, 'Let's just drive; I'll take some Nitro and we'll see how it goes.'"

It didn't.

"I had to take three Nitros."

They didn't work.

"My chest feels like there is a fucking car running over it. I was in extreme pain in the middle of my chest. So we had to U-turn and go back to the hospital."

Frankie was immediately taken up to the cardio unit where they started administering tests to see what was wrong.

"It was the same as the last time, a heart attack, just not as intense. Same thing. They put a stent in and I was OK. I really felt a lot better. But now, I've got one cardiologist in Wisconsin under one name, another in Georgia under a second, and I was 'Frankie Saggio' back here on the Island."

If Frankie said the wrong thing, they'd know something was up. How could the same guy have three doctors in three different states under three different names unless he was a "bad guy?" Frankie would have to lie . . . a little.

"'Where'd you have your first stents put in?' the cardiologist asks me.

"'Mexico,' I said. They still wanted the records. Then I say, 'Listen, I called up for the records and I'm having a very hard time because, you know, the language barrier,' and all this shit. Then I got no medical insurance. If I use my records from Wisconsin—the real records, the actual heart attack—then I have no medical insurance."

Because Dwight had forgotten to buy it for Frankie. It took some time, but Frankie was able to convince the doctors in Winthrop Hospital that his records were unavailable. Which was just as well.

"Turned out, the clog was in a different artery. Yeah; it was clogged a lot more than the first one. So I don't understand how they didn't catch it. The cardiologist recommended an EC study and everything. I had it in Wisconsin. It's like having an angioplasty, but they go in just to look.

"In other words, I had stents and I had the balloon job on the other artery. And then on this one, they had to put two stents in, one in the top and one in the bottom. A stent keeps the artery open. They said the one I had put in is holding up pretty well."

Ironically, because of his age, Frankie wasn't a candidate for the open-heart surgery that would have permanently repaired his heart.

"The problem is, is that I'm too young for the operation. Prime age for the operation is about fifty. If you have the operation at my age, what happens is your heart doesn't have enough arteries around it. You need to be a little bit older. And I don't have those like a fifty-year-old man would have them. I'm a candidate for the operation, but my doctor . . . I've been to three different doctors. Three different doctors tell me three different things."

Which frustrated Frankie to no end.

"The cardiologist told me that the doctor in 'Mexico' should have picked up that I had another blocked artery. I was walking around since the first attack with a time bomb in my chest. That doctor up in Wisconsin that treated me? I would have loved to have worked on his heart a little, make him sniff a little oxygen."

Frankie had not checked in with Barney since arriving in New York.

"I called up Barney. I got his machine. I just left a message. No, I didn't tell him I had another heart attack. I told him my baby was in the hospital, I was in town, and I had probation and everything—boom, boom, boom. So I told him I had called the U.S. Attorney, told the U.S. Attorney I had to come, and this and that and all the other thing.

"Few hours later, I get a pissed off message from Barney on my cell. 'Don't call the U.S. Attorney anymore. Call me back.' But if I don't call the U.S. Attorney, I don't get a quick response because of this terrorist stuff, which is understandable. I lost a friend in the WTC, a civilian fireman. Even in our thing, we never hurt any civilians.

"So I called the U.S. Attorney. They were the only ones anyway who knew what was happening with the cases and if they'd need me in court. I still had a deal with them. Then, I beep Barney and he calls me back.

"'This is Barney,' he says. 'Oh, your baby is in the hospital. Which wife?'

"'Which wife? Which wife? What are you? Out of your fucking mind?' So I started fucking screaming at him. I told him, 'Fuck you, you fucking . . .' I go and I'm fucking pissed off, you know? I've been divorced for eight years! He's an asshole. I start fucking yelling at him and screaming at him, tell him to fuck off and everything else.

"'You really can't be around here, you got to get out of here,' he started telling me. Your security . . .' Then I start, 'Let me tell you something. What fucking security? I haven't had fucking security in fucking two years. I have to fucking call somebody if I needed something, and by that time I'll be stiff as a fucking board. So who are you bullshitting? There was no security. There is none. You know, you got some fucking balls.'"

Frankie was blowing off steam and then some.

"'I'm in the hospital and my baby is in the hospital and he needs a transfusion.' That's when I tell him I had another fucking heart attack and he finally stops butching me. But he tells me, 'Call the U.S. Attorney and let them know that you're around in case they want to see you or anything. And check in with your probation officer.' So I call the fucking probation officer back in Georgia to tell him what was happening.

"'You got drugs in your urine,' he tells me. Periodically, I was getting these drug tests.

"'Listen,' I said, 'I'm on fifteen different pills. What are you trying to tell me?' He's, like, 'Well . . .' I said, 'What? Are you kidding me? My kid is in the hospital, I got to be here, and he's going to be in the hospital for at least three months.'

"'Well, I got to get somebody to watch you there,' he says. So then I called Barney back. I got into it with Barney. I really went fucking nuts. I was screaming at him. I told him, 'Fuck you!' We were just going at it. I was just yelling at him. About a half-hour later I talked to him and he was apologizing. 'I'm sorry,' boom, boom, boom. 'I didn't realize. Because I know you call your daughter your baby sometimes.' He was just full of shit, you know?

"So he said to me, 'What is your son's blood type? We're all tested for AIDS constantly, and we'll get him some blood.' Because I can't give blood because of all the medication that I'm on. See, premature babies get very anemic, so at some point they're going to need transfusions. So actually, yeah, one of the agents did go down and he donated because he's the same blood type as my son."

Besides blood and the runaround, Barney had some concrete advice.

"You've got to be real, real careful. You got to get in and out of there as quick as possible. We don't want you in the area too long."

With good reason. While Frankie wasn't going to any of his former hangouts, it was always possible to run into one of his old acquaintances. But Frankie explains the problem. "My son has got to stay in that hospital for a few months, so that makes it harder."

In January 2002, the baby was doing as well as could be expected after having come into the world a bit early.

"He's got a collapsed lung, but they're trying to straighten that out. Which they said is not uncommon for a ten-week-old that was twenty-six-and-a-half weeks at birth."

Frankie Saggio's post-Mob life was not going as planned. The plan had been to leave Witness Security with a new identity, his wife, and the money he had stashed away from his old identity—just the two of them into a new world outside of New York.

Not quite.

Now, there were three. And it's sort of hard to be on the run with a baby. Richard Kimble knew that; anytime he got close to somebody, he moved on.

How much longer could Frankie stay in the danger zone without Tommy D or Robert Misseri finding out where he was? The longer he stayed in New York, of course, the more difficult it would be to conceal his true identity.

But he couldn't leave: his son needed him. If Frankie Saggio courted death by being at his son's side, then so be it. He'd stay in the danger zone as long as he had to. His Uncle Philly had taught him that you sacrifice everything for family, even your life.

Chapter Fifteen

1970 RESTORED FORD TRUCK

Immediately after the attack on the World Trade Center, the United States Court for the Eastern District of New York suspended operations. No one in New York was capable of doing business and anyone who said they were, was lying.

Bin Laden's bloodthirstiness made even Frankie wary. Like most wiseguys, he cared not a knit for politics but the safety of his family was uppermost always. No one could go anywhere in the New York area for awhile without worrying that the tunnel they were passing through or the bridge they were passing over might suddenly be blown up. In the wake of the traumatic collapse of the twin symbols of the United States economic system, everyone in New York was walking around with post-traumatic stress syndrome, including wiseguys.

As far as the court was concerned, it took a few weeks before they were back in business trying cases. First up on the calendar, of course, were the cases already in progress when the planes hit. The cases that had already been scheduled, including the ones in which Frankie might have to testify, were postponed. The Feds told Frankie they wouldn't come to trial until the late winter of 2002 at the earliest.

From what Barney told Frankie and from what Frankie read in the paper, if even half the guys who were indicted as a result of the information he had given the federal government were eventually convicted, the Mob would be dealt a severe blow. As Frankie went through the doors of Winthrop Hospital, washed up in the neonatal unit, and put on his gown and mask, he determined that his son would have a different life, Frank, Jr. would be the first Saggio not born to the mob.

Hopefully.

As for the two men who wanted him dead, Tommy D was still in custody; no bail for the skipper. Robert Misseri, though, was not regarded with such distrust by the court. He was released on bail pending sentencing and was back on the street.

"The phone rang. I'm at my house on the Island. Aria took the call. Some guy was looking for me. I'm sure it was Robert."

Paranoia or reality? Frankie didn't know.

They would finally move. Despite her difficult pregnancy, Aria had sold their house. They would get over $300,000 for it, that plus what Frankie had put away would give them a nest egg to start their new life free from the Bonannos, free from the Five Families, and free from the government. They needed to leave the danger zone soon.

Life had been a lot simpler when Frankie Saggio was a boy. His uncles were alive and they had shown him the ropes. Everyone had dinner together, everyone laughed and smoked. Everyone shared life events: christenings, weddings, sweet sixteen's, Christmas.

Christmas. Frankie remembered Christmas at his uncle's fondly. But he just didn't get it back then. He thought the Saggios and the Giaccones and the Clemenzas were the same as anyone else. He thought it would all go on forever. He had forgotten that his family was different.

DECEMBER, 2001

Two heart attacks and a premature baby later, Frankie Saggio looked like he hadn't changed much. He was still nattily dressed—a casual blue pullover with a pair of sleek-looking, gray and white warm up pants. Maybe he was a little thinner if you looked close. We were sitting at the kitchen table of a house he had rented in the town of Cold Spring Harbor on the north shore of Long Island.

"Come on buddy, ya gotta eat," said Frankie.

We dug in. Aria Saggio had made a spread like nothing I had ever seen—all different types of Italian cold cuts on so many platters, I lost count, succulent mozzarella in oil and oregano topped with paper thin slices of fresh ripe tomatoes. Crusty bread and lucatella cheese, a wheel of it, and two types of salami, giant green olives and marinated artichoke hearts, topped off with strong coffee and Italian cookies.

Through everything that happened to him, we had talked and talked and talked. It was the second time we were meeting after his heart attack and I knew it would be one of the last. He was getting ready to leave the Island for good.

"So I guess after everything that's happened, you're not going some-place like Utah or Idaho where you can't get your bagel in the morning?" I asked, smiling.

"Definitely not buddy," he answered with what was now his familiar deep throaty laugh. "Actually, I don't know where we're going."

First he had to stand before a judge in the Brooklyn courtroom of the United States Court of the Eastern District of New York and be sentenced on the phony pay phone scam charges. When that was over, he would then have something that his Uncle Philly would have coveted— a new identity but at the terrible price of learning the real truth about life in the mob.

"There's no honor left," said Frankie.

Something made me turn to my left. Three almost floor to ceiling beveled windows covered the far wall and looked out on the street. I could make out the top of a white car that slowly drove past. *Nothing*, I thought.

Frankie walked me out to my car. In the driveway was an absolutely gorgeous, fully restored 1970 Ford Truck.

"You like it buddy?"

"How are you feeling?" I asked bluntly.

He paused before answering.

"I gotta go get some things taken care of," he said, dragging with pleasure on a Marlboro Black. "They gotta do, I think another stent."

I looked around. The street was quiet, motionless. I drove away hoping I'd see him again.

Five months went by. I heard nothing from him and was beginning to believe that despite Frankie's assurances about the Mulberry Street guys, they could find him and might already have, which might account for the time lapse. Meanwhile, in the papers, wiseguys were coming to trial right and left. What I didn't know was that Frankie was busy talking.

MAY 22, 2002

Robert Misseri was on the line. It was obvious it was him from the moment he spoke. The fast talking, Long Island patter that Frankie had warned me about made it obvious who it was. Using the name "Michael Boss," what police refer to as an "A.K.A.," he stated that he had a company called "Artists and Acquisitions."

Robert claimed that he was working with Sam Wunderkind, a midsized book publisher. Robert was extremely polite. He was calling, he said, to see about optioning the rights to any book Frankie might be thinking about writing about his life.

"Who told you Frankie might be thinking of doing a book?"

"I don't want to say."

"He's not interested in any movie deal," said Frankie, when he was told of Robert's latest activities. "He wants to see if I'm going to write anything about him that the Feds can use against him when his sentencing comes up, which is soon."

A call to Sam Wunderkind confirmed that he knew Misseri and was allowing him to hang around his publishing offices to develop properties. But he had no idea that Misseri was under indictment for his fraudulent activities as Frankie's partner on the pay phone scam. Ironically, Frankie had gone up to Sam Wunderkind's midtown offices to pitch Sam's editor-in-chief on a book about his life. When he did, Frankie had no idea that he was literally yards away from Misseri. Neither, supposedly, did Misseri, who probably found out about the proposed book through office gossip.

"Just another way wiseguys get into businesses," Frankie explained. "If Robert started making money with Sam Wunderkind, the bosses would start expecting it from Sam on a regular basis."

JUNE 3, 2002

A press release from the NYS Attorney General's Office began in a surprisingly succinct manner:

17 Associates of the Gambino Organized Crime Family Indicted

Individuals Used Extortion, Wire Fraud and Witness Tampering to Control Waterfront Businesses

State Attorney General Eliot Spitzer and federal and state authorities today announced the arrests and indictments of 17 members and associate of the Gambino Organized Crime Family of La Cosa Nostra for racketeering, extortion, wire-fraud, loan sharking, operating illegal gambling businesses, money laundering, witness tampering and other related crimes.

Among the seventeen indicted, one name stood out: Julius Nasso. As Julius R. Nasso, he had been the producing partner of martial arts movie star Steven Seagal since the 1990 hackneyed potboiler *Marked For Death*. *Out For Justice* (1991), *On Deadly Ground* (1994), *Under Siege 2: Dark Territory* (1995), *The Glimmer Man* (1996), *Fire Down Below* (1997) and *The Patriot* (1998) are all Seagal films, all bearing Nasso's producer credit. Nasso had such a close relationship with his producing partner that Seagal latter actually bought a home on Staten Island near Nasso's to be close to his buddy. Then it all changed.

The indictment also charges that beginning in September 2000 and continuing through May 2002 . . . [Anthony] Ciccone, [Primo] Cassarino, V. [Vincent] Nasso and Julius Nasso attempted to extort a well-known movie star and film director.

The "well-known movie star and film director" the indictment refers to is Seagal. The indictment continues:

The defendants attempted to use Ciccone's position as a captain in the Gambino family to pressure the victim to pay them money or to include J. Nasso in the victim's next film project. In one incident, the victim was directed to pay Ciccone $165,000 for each film he made.

Seagal would later deny that despite his long business relationship with Nasso, he ever in any way, shape or form, knew of Nasso's alleged Mob associations. Frankie, though, has a different take.

"Let's say a guy needs money. That happens all the time. But let's say this time, it's an actor who needs the money to make a movie. It's the kind of deal where someone says to the star, 'You come up with fifty percent and we [the studio], will put up the other fifty.'"

This kind of deal is SOP in the movie business and allows more than one business entity to split the risk of producing a movie.

"Now let's say the star is friends with a guy who's connected. The guy goes to his skipper to get the money but this is a big deal because if the star's movie hits, then the wiseguys have got their hooks into him. And let's say, that's exactly what happens.

"That first movie, financed partially with mob money, goes on to be a hit. Now the bosses want their cut on every movie this star does. After all, they have helped make him a star, why shouldn't they have a piece of everything he does? And that's okay with the star. For awhile, he's making it hand over fist. But then suddenly, lo and behold what do you think happens buddy?

"The star's not popular any more. Turns out, everyone thinks the guy's a shit and not a stand-up guy. And no one goes to see his movies any more. But the bosses still want their cut. Makes no difference whether the movies do business or not. The bosses have to get theirs.

"By now, the star is losing money. He's really bleeding. What do you think is the best way out of owing a debt to us? I'll tell you what buddy, say you were extorted. Tell the government that and *bam*, you're off the hook. You don't owe anybody nothing no more.

The case against Nasso is still pending.

DECEMBER, 2002

Before a Federal witness goes into court to testify, the prosecution spends weeks, sometimes months prepping him. Since witnesses in the RICO cases against members of the Outfit frequently involve what are euphemistically described by the tabloid media as "turncoat witnesses." In Uncle Jimmy's era, they were known as "canaries."

It really wasn't necessary in Misseri's case for Frankie to be briefed for more than a few weeks. The government had already gotten their plea from Misseri. There hadn't even been a trial. When you have a murder indictment hanging over a defendant and you offer to drop it in return for a plea, it's amazing how fast you can make a deal.

That the cycle was now complete was not a detail that Frankie ignored. That he was the first member of his family to turn against the Mob family that had been his home his whole life, was not a fact that escaped him. At night when he'd go outside and smoke a cigarette—one of many he would have during the day, it was a habit he just couldn't kick despite his heart condition—he thought about it.

Fuck it. Fuck *them*. They had tried to kill him. There was no more contract.

The United States Court for the Eastern District of New York has thirteen active judges, seven senior judges and thirteen magistrate judges. The district comprises the counties of Kings, Queens, Richmond and Suffolk. Because Frankie and Robert's crime had been committed in Suffolk, the Eastern District had jurisdiction.

Frankie found himself at the Cadman Plaza Federal courthouse in downtown Brooklyn, not too far from Bensonhurst. This was definitely the "danger zone," which was why he was closely guarded by Federal agents who hustled him into the courthouse to testify at Misseri's pre-sentencing hearing.

It was of course no surprise to Misseri that it was Frankie who helped build the indictment and ultimately his conviction. He knew and so did his lawyers. "They had me testify basically to our whole relationship, from start to finish. I was in that courtroom eight hours a day for a full week testifying. I made sure to make eye contact with Robert so he'd know I didn't fear him. He looked back at me, but he couldn't react too strongly because the judge was looking at him," Frankie recalls.

At the end of the hearing, Misseri was sentenced to two years in prison. Eligible for parole in 2005, he is serving his time at Allenwood, a low security federal prison in White Deer, PA.

AFTERWORD

Frankie got himself a new life and a new job. He did what he said he was going to do—he went straight.

First, Frankie moved his family out of New York. Using the experience of his Wall Street days, Frankie set up a boiler room.

"What I got buddy is a large room," he said over the phone. "Got about ten or eleven desks covering the walls lined up next to each other and on top of each is a brand new Dell Pentium IV with seventeen-inch flat screen monitor."

Frankie gave the investment counselors he hired leads on investors and later would represent the firm at investor gatherings. "I'm not using Saggio," he explained, "but my new name. Nobody knows who I am. To them, I'm just some financial analyst."

Even in his new business, Frankie couldn't break emotionally free from the old one. The giveaway was Frankie's complete lack of trust in his fellows. He had absolutely none, and he acted that way. Paid by a legitimate vendor by check for example, Frankie rushed to the vendor's bank to cash the check. He wanted *cash*. It's the best thing to have when you're on the run.

Aria had given birth to their second child. Frankie was happy now, with his wife and children, living someplace in Bush's America like a millennium version of *Leave it to Beaver's* "the Cleavers." And that didn't make sense, not because it was an antiquated ideal but because the truth was so different.

Why could Frankie defraud honest people without giving it a second thought? Why was it that wiseguys can go from being the nicest guys one minute to cold blooded killers the next? Is there something in the Castellemare Del Golfo waters that fuels the rage? Or is it something else?

Frankie grew up in a home where his parents were nothing but loving. But all around him was the background noise of violence. It was not only tolerated by his family, it was encouraged. There was never any attempt by his parents to dissociate from the Mob side of the family.

Only Philly Lucky knew how bad the life really was. Had he not been murdered, he would have made certain Frankie and his son Philip, Jr. did not go into the Mob. They were his second chance, to make good on a life that had started so promisingly and then been destroyed when he joined the Bonannos.

Nobody starts out a killer except maybe the most genetically aberrant psychopath. Frankie had not crossed that line, yet, of murdering a fellow human being. But the very pragmatic, almost fatalistic view of life that wiseguys adopt made them particularly prone to engaging in violence because, sooner or later, it was going to happen. And it did. For that reason, Frankie always kept his shiny flat automatic with him wherever he went, snug up against his hip.

The knowledge that violence lies below the surface, always there, festering, and can boil over into rage at a moment's notice, keeps mobsters on constant edge. Frankie remembers a funeral procession he was a part of, snaking through the Bronx. A family member was being taken for burial to the cemetery when a rude bus driver cut into the line of autos with their lights on, the traditional sign of funeral traffic. Frankie's relatives got out of their car, stopped the bus, got on and began beating the bus driver senseless for his mistake. They didn't think twice about it.

As for the Feds, they kept Frankie on a tight leash. Frankie would only be free of them when he was sentenced. They were delaying that as long as they could, so Frankie could continue helping them put cases together.

AUGUST, 2003

Julius Nasso decided to make a deal. He pled guilty to extortion conspiracy in return for a year in jail and a $150,000 fine. He told the court that he used a Gambino Family connection to threaten Seagal, the former action star, into coughing up money he said he owed him because of their business relationship. I called Frankie to discuss the deal, but I couldn't reach him. He contacted me a week later.

"Hey buddy, the reason I haven't called you for awhile, was we had to go out of town for awhile. Some problems with the 'G'" said Frankie's voice on the answering machine. The "G" he was referring to meant the government.

"It was about a month ago and the doorbell rings where I'm livin.' I asked on the intercom who it is.

"'It's Barney.'

"I'm thinking, 'Holy shit, what's he doin' comin' to *my house* where I got my wife and kids?' So he comes in all hangdog.

"'Frankie, I'm really sorry,' he says, 'but someone got into our computer down at the federal parole office. We're not sure who it is. They've gotten access to the files of some of the guys like you.'

"I couldn't fucking believe it. You should see the security in the place; they wouldn't even let me bring in my cell phone. So they moved us for awhile, out of town, until they were sure everything was okay."

But they still hadn't figured out who had done it or what they were doing with the information.

"It really makes you wonder," Frankie said with characteristic understatement. He couldn't get over somebody compromising government security and thus putting the lives of his family and himself in danger.

Frankie Saggio was facing some very real dangers. Both Tommy D and Robert Misseri would be out of jail in a short while. No matter his nonchalance, Frankie knew better than to underestimate them. The thought never left Frankie's mind that he was still born to the mob and always would be.

GLOSSARY

Agita: Angst, trouble.

Away: The time that a gangster is gone serving his time in prison.

Bad guys: Police-speak for criminals.

Bit: The minimum prison sentence served before parole.

Bitch: A prisoner who is forced to sodomize another prisoner.

Blow: Cocaine.

Bocci: An Italian game played with little black balls.

Boss: The head of a Crime Family.

Box, the: Solitary confinement.

Bullpen: The holding cells at a courthouse.

Butch in: Trying to take over somebody's action.

Button: Becoming a made guy, as in "getting your button."

Button Man: A killer.

Capo: A captain of a crew of cutthroat mobsters.

Clip: Murder.

Cojones: Testicles.

Commission, the: The bosses of the Five Families who meet to conduct business and make decisions; the "Justice League" of the Mob.

Consigliere: The top adviser to the boss.

Courts: Areas in the prison yard segregated by race and ethnic group.

Crew: A specific group of gangsters who work for a capo and have regular meetings.

Earner: A mobster who makes money for his capo.

Fed: An agent from the FBI.

Fence-Jumpers: Mobsters who go from one Family to another.

Flipping: When a wiseguy makes a plea bargain agreement with the government.

Hook: The guy who can fence the goods.

Horse Room: Before off-track betting, it was an illegal place to wager on horse races.

In the life: Being a gangster and all that goes with the lifestyle.

Juice: Respect.

Kick up: The cut the skipper gets from his underlings' businesses.

Lay Up: Stay jailed.

Maytag: The same as a bitch.

Omerta: Silence, under the penalty of death.

On the pad: On the take; someone who is being bribed.

Pinched: Arrested.

Primer: The guy who gets the cash tap flowing.

Shylock: A loan shark.

Skipper: The same as a capo.

Soldier: A crew member.

Taste: The cost of doing business: what you have to kick back to your capo.

Throwaways: Guns with the serial number filed off so they can't be traced.

Vig: The usurious interest loan sharks charge.

Wiseguy: A guy in the Mob.

Yards, the: The general prison population.

Zips: Gangsters from Italy.

Connecticut Bell, Inc. was one of Frankie's pay phone scams. Here are some elements of the press kit that he used to sell his phantom pay phone routes.

CT

Connecticut Bell Inc.

6 Landmark Square 4ᵗʰ Floor-Stamford, C.T. 06901
Phone (203)359-5777 Toll Free (888)869-9995
Website: www.ctbell.com

BENEFITS OF THE PRIVATE PAYPHONE BUSINESS

1. *Immediate Cash Flow.*

2. *Freedom to Be Your Own Boss.*

3. *All Cash Business.*

4. *Flexible Hours with Lots of Time Off.*

5. *No Personal Selling Required.*

6. *No Employees to Pay.*

7. *Repeat Business.*

8. *Part - Time of Full - Time.*

9. *Easy to Start - Up.*

Western Bell Inc.
701 North Green Valley Pkwy. Suite 200
Henderson, NV 89014
Phone (702) 990-3236 • Fax (702) 990-3001
Offices Located Nationwide
In North Carolina Call 1 800 377 4030

TAX BENEFITS

As a Distributor, you may write off through depreciation the total purchase price of the equipment, usually over a period of 3-5 years. This benefit is also known **"cost recovery"**.

In addition, and is most important as it goes on and on, Distributors are allowed **tax deductions** for expenses incurred in generating and collecting income and in operating and servicing the equipment.

Besides direct expenses, the business portion of the following costs can be deducted from your gross **income**.

HOUSE	AUTO
House Payments or Rent	Gas and Oil
Taxes and Insurance	Repairs
Telephone	Insurance
Electricity, Gas and Water	Depreciation
Repairs and Maintenance	Licenses
Depreciation (if owned)	

KEOGH PLAN - TAX BONUS

Since you must own your business to make this tax deduction
(up to **$30,000**), this valuable tax savings is yours!

See your CPA or accountant for verification to your own individual tax situation.

TAX BENEFITS

As a Distributor, you may write off through depreciation the total purchase price of the equipment, usually over a period of 3-5 years. This benefit is also known **"cost recovery"**.

In addition, and is most important as it goes on and on, Distributors are allowed **tax deductions** for expenses incurred in generating and collecting income and in operating and servicing the equipment.

Besides direct expenses, the business portion of the following costs can be deducted from your gross **income.**

HOUSE	AUTO
House Payments or Rent	Gas and Oil
Taxes and Insurance	Repairs
Telephone	Insurance
Electricity, Gas and Water	Depreciation
Repairs and Maintenance	Licenses
Depreciation (if owned)	

KEOGH PLAN - TAX BONUS
Since you must own your business to make this tax deduction (up to **$30,000**), this valuable tax savings is yours!

See your CPA or accountant for verification to your own individual tax situation.

Western Bell Inc.

701 North Green Valley Pkwy. Suite 200
Henderson, NV 89014
Phone (702) 990-3236 • Fax (702) 990-3001
Offices Located Nationwide

BENEFITS OF THE PRIVATE PAYPHONE BUSINESS

1. *Immediate Cash Flow.*

2. *Freedom to Be Your Own Boss.*

3. *All Cash Business.*

4. *Flexible Hours with Lots of Time Off.*

5. *No Personal Selling Required.*

6. *No Employees to Pay.*

7. *Repeat Business.*

8. *Part - Time of Full - Time.*

9. *Easy to Start - Up.*

10. *Secure Future.*

FINANCING GROWTH PLAN

TO OUR ESTABLISHED DISTRIBUTORS

AS SOON AS YOU'RE COMFORTABLE IN YOUR NEW BUSINESS AND READY TO EXPAND,

We Are Ready To Help!

**AFTER ALL,
YOUR SUCCESS IS OUR SUCCESS!**

We Welcome Your Questions

1-800-796-8322

QUESTIONS & ANSWERS

The local telecommunications market generates over $86 billion dollars annually. In an August 1992 ruling, the Federal Communications Commission voted to open a $300 million slice of the phone service pie to private competition.[1]

Since 1984, when the break up of the AT & T monopoly was ordered, small companies have consistently gained access to private phone lines for business customers.[2]

Now **CT BELL** is able to offer the small business person the opportunity to capitalize on the booming telecommunications industry.

Q. WHERE ARE PRIVATE PAYPHONES LOCATED?

A. They are located in high traffic public places including: Hotels, bars and restaurants, laundromats, college dorms, hospitals, beauty salons, auto repair shops, truck stops, strip malls, convenient stores, factories and bowling alleys.

Q. HOW MANY HOURS A WEEK DOES SERVICING A TELEPHONE ROUTE TAKE?

A. Obviously, it depends on how many telephones you purchase and how widely spread out your locations are. But, servicing – which consists of coin collection and only nominal maintenance, along with the light bookkeeping that a cash business requires – is definitely within the bounds of part-time employment.

Q. WHO IS THE BUSINESS RIGHT FOR?

A. Our client profile varies widely. It's a perfect business opportunity for husbands wanting to buy their wives a small business, for women with children desiring part-time income, retired persons wishing to supplement, fixed incomes, college students wanting part-time employment income while they are studying, persons interested in becoming self-employed on weekends or after work, or those looking to become self-employed for the, first time. In other words, this business is suitable for anyone, aged 18 to 80, who is self-motivated and who desires additional income combined with the flexibility to set their own schedule.

Q. HOW DOES THE PAYPHONE INDUSTRY COMPARE WITH OTHER VENDING BUSINESS OPPORTUNITIES?

A. We have found our potential clients are sometimes investigating other vending opportunities such as soda or candy machines. Private payphones are a much simpler product to manage. Typically, a soda or candy vending business need much more servicing: Ordering the product, restocking, servicing the product and equipment, and dealing with spoilage. Additionally, one must buy or rent extra equipment such as hand trucks, carts, vans, dollies, refrigeration and/or storage facilities. With payphones, you have none of that trouble or expense.

Q. WILL **CT BELL** FINANCE MY EXPANSION?

A. It is CT Bell's goal to see you succeed. You can expand at your own pace. CT Bell Payphone Distributors, will finance your expansion with 0% interest. This is no income verification financing, therefore prudence requires us to ask for a down-payment of 50% for financed payphones. The term for our financing is based on the type and number of payphones purchased. Financing is for existing clients only.

Q. CAN **CT BELL** PROVIDE EXTENDED WARRANTY?

A. All customers can purchase an extra three years on All phones purchased.

Q. ARE THERE ANY TAX BENEFITS?

A. As a private payphone owner, you may write off through depreciation the total purchase price of the equipment usually over a period of 3-5 years

In addition, and this is most important as it goes on and on payphone owners are allowed tax deductions for expenses incurred in generating and collecting income and in operating and servicing the equipment.

Besides the direct expense, the business portion of the following costs can be deducted from your gross income.

HOUSE House Payments or Rent • Taxes and Insurance
Telephone • Electricity, Gas and Water
Repairs and Maintenance • Depreciation (if owned)

AUTO Gas and Oil • Repairs • Insurance
Depreciation • Licenses

KEOGH PLAN - TAX BONUS
Since you must own your own business to make this tax deduction (up to $30,000), this valuable tax savings is yours!
See your CPA or accountant for verification and application to your own individual tax situation

1 Ramirez, A., The New York Times, August 6, 1993,Vol. 142, p D2
2 Ramirez, A., The New York Times, August 4, 1993,Vol. 142, p C1

SOFTWARE MANAGEMENT

TELELINK FOR WINDOWS

Managing your phone route can be quite time-consuming. Very few owners have enogh hours in the day to personally check each location. Fortunately, Ernest Telecom's *Telelink* software management package allows you to "visit" each location as often as you like through the power of a personal computer. Furthermore, Ernest Telecom's *Telelink for Windows* breaks new ground in the payphone industry by offering the first Windows-based software management package. Telelink for Windows allows you to:

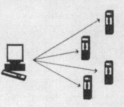

• Program and monitor installed pay phones from the privacy and comfort of your home or office.

• Generates reports for commission statements, revenue analysis, and maintenence orders.

• Complete multiple tasks on your computer simultaneously.

• Utilize the full capabilities of the program quickly and efficiently because of the ease of Windows.

• Manage your route more effectively through the use of extensive programmable features.

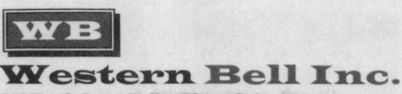

APPENDIX II

Frankie Saggio's federal indictment, including extensive details about the pay phone scam.

```
GAS: JMM: jmm
F.#19999R00617
SAGGIO. INF
```

```
UNITED STATES DISTRICT COURT
EASTERN DISTRICT OF NEW YORK
- - - - - - - - - - - - - - - - -X
UNITED STATES OF AMERICA

     — against —

FRANK SAGGIO,

                    Defendant.
- - - - - - - - - - - - - - - - -X
```

I N F O R M A T I O N

Cr. No._____
(T. 18, U.S.C., §§
1341, 1344(1), 2 and
3551 et sea.)

THE UNITED STATES ATTORNEY CHARGES:

At various times relevant to this information:

Count One

1. The defendant FRANK SAGGIO directed and participated in the day-to-day operations of American Paytel, Inc. ("American Paytel"), a New York corporation located at 1111 Route 110, Suite 351, Melville, New York.

2. In [sic] or about and between January 1997 and December 1997, both dates being approximate and inclusive, within the Eastern District of New York and elsewhere, the defendant FRANK SAGGIO, together with others, knowingly and intentionally devised a scheme and artifice to defraud American Paytel customers and to obtain money and property from American Paytel customers by means of false and fraudulent pretenses, representations and prom-

ises, and for the purpose of executing such scheme and artifice used or caused to be used the United States mail.

3. It was part of the scheme and artifice that the defendant FRANK SAGGIO, together with others, placed advertisements in publications, including "Pennysavers," that were delivered by United States mail. These advertisements solicited individuals to purchase payphones form American Paytel, as well as locations, known as "routes," from which these payphones could be operated and promised profits to individuals from the operation, when, as the defendant FRANK SAGGIO well knew and believed, he and other participants in the scheme did not intend to deliver payphones and routes to these individuals.

3. It was part of the scheme and artifice that the defendant FRANK SAGGIO, together with others, placed advertisements in publications, including "Pennysaver", that were delivered by United States mail. These advertisements solicited individuals to purchase payphones from American Paytel, as well as locations, known as "routes," from which these payphones could be operated, and promised profits to individuals from the operation, when, as the defendant FRANK SAGGIO well knew and believed, he and other participants in the scheme did not intend to deliver payphones and routes to these individuals.

4. It was further part of the scheme and artifice that the defendant FRANK SAGGIO spoke with potential American Paytel customers over the telephone and in person and represented to them that American Paytel would provide payphones and routes, whereas, as he well knew and believed, no such equipment and routes would be provided.

5. It was further part of the scheme and artifice that the defendant FRANK SAGGIO, together with others,

received payments in the form of cash, checks, stocks and property from individuals for the purchase of payphones and routes.

6. It was further part of the scheme and artifice that the defendant FRANK SAGGIO, together with others, after collecting these payments from American Paytel customers, did not provide equipment and routes to them but used these payments for personal purposes.

7. For the purpose of executing the scheme and artifice, on or about the date set forth below, within the Eastern District of New York, the defendant FRANK SAGGIO did knowingly place and cause to be placed in an author-

Approximate Mailing Date	Description	Recipient
2/17/97	A "Pennysaver" newspaper containing an American Paytel advertisement and solicitation	John Doe Oyster Bay, New York

ized depository for mail matter to be delivered by the United States Postal Service, and knowingly caused to be delivered by mail, according to the directions thereon, the following mail matter:

(Title 18, United States Code, Sections 1341, 2 and 3551 et seq.)

Count Two

8. The defendant FRANK SAGGIO directed and participated in the day-to-day operations of New England Pay Telephone Corporation, Inc., which conducted business under the name United Pay Telephone, Inc. ("United") a New York corporation located at One EAB Plaza, Suite 165, Uniondale, New York.

9. In [sic] or about October 1997, the defendant FRANK SAGGIO opened and caused the opening of a corporate

NEW ENGLAND PAY TELEPHONE CORP.
DBA UNITED PAY TELEPHONE
1016
188
DATE 3/26/98
PAY TO THE ORDER OF CASH $9,500.00
Nine Thousand Five Hundred   DOLLARS
EAB EAB Plaza New York 11555
FOR

NEW ENGLAND PAY TELEPHONE CORP.
DBA UNITED PAY TELEPHONE
165 EAB PLAZA
UNIONDALE, NY 11556-0165
1300
188
DATE 1/20/98
PAY TO THE ORDER OF Frank Saggio $900.00
Nine Hundred   DOLLARS
EAB EAB Plaza New York 11555
FOR

checking account in the name of United at a branch of the EAB Bank, a financial institution the deposits of which were insured by the Federal Deposit Insurance Corporation, located at One EAB Plaza, Uniondale, New York (hereinafter referred to as "the EAB account").

10. On or about and between January 21, 1998 and January 26, 1998, both dates being approximate and inclusive, within the Eastern District of New York and elsewhere, the defendant FRANK SAGGIO did knowingly and intentionally execute and attempt to execute a scheme and artifice to defraud EAB and Key Bank, another financial institution the deposits of which were insured by the federal Deposit Insurance Corporation, located at 49 North Franklin Street, Hempstead, New York."

11. It was a part of the scheme and artifice that the defendant FRANK SAGGIO solicited individuals to purchase payphones from United, as well as locations, known as "routes," from which these pay telephones could be operated. Although individuals were promised profits from the operation of the payphones, as the defendant FRANK SAGGIO well knew and believed, he and other participants in the scheme did not intend to deliver payphones and routes, and therefore there would not be profits to individuals who paid the defendant for such telephones and routes"

12. It was further part of the scheme and artifice that, on or about January 21, 1998, the defendant FRANK SAGGIO caused the deposit into the EAB account of a personal check of a United customer, in the amount of $10,000. This check, when initially credited to the EAB account, created a balance of approximately $11,339.92.

13. It was further part of the scheme and artifice that, on or about January 26, 1998, the defendant FRANK SAGGIO withdrew funds from the EAB account in the approximate amount of $10,400 through the use of a cash with-

drawal and the issuance of a United check made payable to the defendant FRANK SAGGIO, knowing that the checked described in paragraph 12, above, was about to be dishonored by the issuer, that payphones and routes would not be provided to the United customer and that once-the $10,000 check was dishonored, these withdrawals would exceed the actual available balance in the EAB account. Later that same day, Key Bank in fact stopped payment on the $10, 000 check, which was then dishonored by Key Bank.

14. It was a further part of the scheme and artifice that the defendant FRANK SAGGIO used the funds obtained as a result of this scheme and artifice for personal expenses.

(Title 18, United States Code, Sections 1344(1), 2 and 3551 et sea.)

LORETTA E. LYNCH
UNITED STATES ATTORNEY
EASTERN DISTRICT OF NEW YORK

1 EAB Plaza, Uniondale, New York 11555 - 2855
The Item(s) listed below which were transacted against your account   18d021562. have been returned unpaid. We have charged your
account on   01/26/98   and   HAVE ENCLOSED THE ITEM(S) LISTED

REASON	DESCRIPTION		AMOUNT
REFER TO MAKER	MAKERS ACCT: 795011366		10,000.00

NEW ENGLAND PAY TELEPHONE CORP
C O UNITED PAY TELEPHONE
D/B/A UNITED PAY TELEPHONE
165 EAB PLAZA WEST TWR.6TH F
UNIONDALE NY   11556

		SERVICE CHARGE	10.00
		TOTAL AMOUNT	10,010.00

0005   0D   9,061.08 DR   V   188

370/0172 OCT 91 1/UNIT

APPENDIX III

The Cooperation Agreement Frankie Saggio negotiated with the federal government.

GAS: JMM: jmm
F. # 1998R00559
saggio.agr

UNITED STATES DISTRICT COURT   <u>COOPERATION AGREEMENT</u>
EASTERN DISTRICT OF NEW YORK

- - - - - - - - - - - - - - - - -X

UNITED STATES OP AMERICA

    — against —

FRANK SAGGIO,

                   Defendant.

- - - - - - - - - - - - - - - - -X

Pursuant to RUlc 11 of the Federal Rule of Criminal Procedure, the United States Attorney's Office for the Eastern District of New York (the office") and FRANK SAGGIO (the "defendant") agree to the following:

1. The defendant will waive indictment and plead guilty to a two-count information to be filed in this district charging violations of 18 U.SC. SS 1341 and 1344. The counts carries the following statutory penalties:

Count One

    a. Maximum term of imprisonment: 5 years (18 U.S.C. S 1341).

    b. Minimum term of imprisonment: 0 years (18 U.S.C. S 1341).

    c. Maximum supervised release term: 3 years, to follow any term of imprisonment; if a condition of release is violated, the defendant may be sentenced to up to 2 years without credit for pre-release imprisonment or time previously served on post-release supervision(18 U.S.C, SS 3583 (b), (e))

d. Maximum fine: $250,000, or twice the pecuniary gain, whichever is greater (18 U.S.C. SS 1341, 3571 (b) (4) and 3571 (d)).

e. Restitution; To be determined by the Court (18 U.S.C. S 3663).

f. $100 special assessment (18 U.S.C. S 3013).

g. Other penalties: N/A.

Count Two

a. Maximum term of imprisonment: 30 years (18 U.S.C. S 1344).

b. Minimum term of imprisonment: 0 year (18 U.S.C. S 1344).

c. Maximum supervised release term: 5 years, to follow any term of imprisonment; if a condition of release is violated, the defendant may be sentenced to up to 3 years without credit for pre-release imprisonment or time previously served on post-release supervision (18 U.S.C. SS 3583 (b), (e)).

d. Maxium fine: $1,000,000 or twice the pecuniary gain, whichever is greater (18 U.S.C, SS 1341, 3571 (b)) (4) and 3571 (d)).

e. Restitution: To be determined by the Court (18 U.S.C. S 3663).

f. $100 special assessment(18 U.S.C. S 3013).

g. Other penalties: N/A.

2. The defendant's sentence is governed by the United States Sentencing Guidelines. The Office will advise the

Court and the Probation Department of information relevant to sentencing, including all criminal activity engaged in by the defendant, and such information may be used by the Court in determining the defendant's sentence. Based on information known to it now, the Office will not oppose a downward adjustment of three levels for acceptance of responsibility under U.S.S.G. S 3E1.1 .

3. The defendant will provide truthful, complete and accurate information and will cooperate fully with the Office. This cooperation will include, but is not limited to, the following:

a. The defendant agrees to be fully debriefed and to attend all meetings at which his presence is requested, concerning his participation in and knowledge of all criminal activities.

b. The defendant agrees to furnish to the Office all documents and other material that may be relevant to the investigation and that are in the defendant's possession or control and to participate in undercover activities pursuant to the specific instructions of law enforcement agents or this Office.

c. The defendant agrees not to reveal a cooperation, or any information derived therefrom, to any third party without prior consent of the Office.

d. The defendant agrees to testify at any proceeding in the Eastern District of New York or elsewhere as requested by the Office

e. The defendant consents to adjournments of his sentence as requested by the Office.

4. The Office agrees that:

a. Except as provided in paragraphs 1, 8, and 9, no further criminal charges will be brought against the defendant for his heretofore disclosed participation in criminal activity involving the following: conspiracy to defraud and use of the mails and wires to defraud others in connection with tile operation c,! American Paytel, United Paytel and American Cigar, Inc., and the unauthorized use of access devices in connection with the operation of A-1 Diamond Exchange all from the period January 1997 to January 1998; the unauthorized use of access devices, bank fraud and the possession and uttering of counterfeit securities involving Credit Services, Inc., Fleet, Key Bank, EAB Bank, Sun Trust Bank of Florida, American Express, Teacher's Federal Credit Union, and Citibank, all from the period January 1995 through December 1996; extortion and assault and conspiracy to commit same against two victims previously identified in or about and between January 1996 and December 1996; robbery of Porto Mare Restaurant, Bayshore, New York, in or about 1996; possession with intent to distribute cocaine and marijuana and conspiracy to commit same all from the period January 1988 and December 1989.

b. No statements made by the defendant during the course of this cooperation will be used against him except as provided in paragraphs 2, 8, and 9.

5. The defendant agrees that the Office may meet with and debrief him without the presence of counsel, unless

the defendant specifically requests counsel's presence at such debriefings and meetings. Upon request of the defendant, the Office will endeavor to provide advance notice to counsel of the place and time of meetings and debriefings, it being understood that the Office's ability to provide such notice will vary according to time constraints and other circumstances. The Office may accommodate requests to alter the time and place of such debriefings. It is understood, however, that any cancellations or reschedulings of debriefing or meetings requested by the defendant that hinder the Office's ability to prepare adequately for trials, hearings or other proceedings may adversely affect the defendant's ability to provide substantial assistance. Matter occurring at any meeting or debriefing may be considered by the Office in determining whether the defendant has provided substantial assistance or otherwise complied with this agreement and may be considered by the court in imposing sentence regardless of whether counsel was present at the meeting or debriefing.

6. If the Office determine that the defendant has cooperated fully, provided substantial assistance to law enforcement authorities and otherwise complied with the terms of this agreement, the Office will file a motion pursuant to U.S.S.G.. S 5Kl.1 and 18 U.S.C. S 3553 (e) with the sentencing Court setting forth the nature and extent of his cooperation. Such a motion will permit the Court, in its discretion, to impose a sentence below the applicable Sentencing Guidelines range and also below any applicable mandatory minimum sentence. In this connection, it is understood that a good faith determination by the Office as to whether the defendant has cooperated fully and provided substantial assistance and has otherwise complied with the terms of this agreement, and the Office's good faith assessment of the value, truthful-

ness, completeness and accuracy of the cooperation, shall be binding upon him. The defendant agrees that, in making this determination, the Office may consider facts known to it at this time. The Office will not recommend to the Court a specific sentence to be posed. Further, the Office cannot and does not make a promise or representation as to what sentence will be imposed by the Court.

7. The defendant agrees that with respect to all charges referred to in paragraphs 1 and 4 (a) he is not a prevailing party within the meaning of the "Hyde Amendment," Section 617, P.L. 105-119 (Nov. 26, 1997), and will not file any claim under that law. The defendant waives any right to additional disclosure from the government in connection with the guilty plea. The defendant agrees to pay the special assessment by check payable to the Clerk of the Court at or before sentencing.

8. The defendant must at all times give complete, truthful, and accurate information and testimony, and must not commit, or attempt to commit, any further crimes. should it be judged by the Office that the defendant has failed to cooperate fully, has intentionally given false, misleading or incomplete information or testimony, has committed or attempted to commit any further crimes, or has otherwise violated any provision of this agreement, the defendant will not be released from his plea of guilty but this Office will be released from its obligations under this agreement, including (a) not to oppose a downward adjustment of three levels for acceptance of responsibility described in paragraph 2 above, and (b) to file the motion described in paragraph 6 above. Moreover, this Office may withdraw the motion described in paragraph 6 above, if such motion has been filed prior to sentencing. The defendant will also be subject to prosecution for any federal criminal violation of which the Office has knowledge, including, but not limited to, the criminal activity

described in paragraph 4 above, perjury and obstruction of justice.

9. Any prosecution resulting from the defendant's failure to comply with the terms of this agreement may be premised upon, among other things: (a) any statements made by the defendant to the Office or to other law enforcement agents on or after June 29, 1998; (b) any testimony given by him before any grand jury or other tribunal, whether before or after the date this agreement is signed by the defendant; and (c) any leads derived from such statements or testimony. Prosecutions that are riot time-barred by the applicable statutes of limitation on the date this agreement is signed may be commenced against the defendant in accordance with this paragraph, notwithstanding the expiration of the statutes of limitation between the signing of this agreement and the commencement of any such prosecutions, Furthermore, the defendant waives all claims under the United States Constitution, Rule 11 (e) (6) of the Federal Rules of Criminal Procedure, Rule 410 of the Federal Rules of Evidence, or any other federal statute or rule, that statements made by him on or after June 29, 1998, or any leads derived therefrom, should be suppressed.

10. If the defendant requests, and in the Office's judgement the request is reasonable, the Office will make application and recommend that the defendant and, if appropriate, other individuals be placed in the Witness Security Program, it being understood that the Office has authority only to recommend and that the final decision to place an applicant in the Witness Security Program rests woth the Department of Justice, which will make its decision in accordance with applicable Departmental regulations.

11. This agreement does not bind any federal, state, or local prosecuting authority other than the Office, and

does not prohibit the Office from initiating and prosecuting any civil or administrative proceedings directly or indirectly involving the defendant.

12. No promises, agreements or conditions have been entered into other than those set forth in this agreement, and none will be entered into unless memorialized in writing and signed by all parties. This agreement supersedes any prior promises, agreements or conditions between the parties. To become effective, this agreement must be signed by all signatries listed below.

Dated: Uniondale, New York

October, 1999

Respectfully submitted,

LORETTA E. LYNCH
United States Attorney
Eastern District of New York

By: _____
James M. Miskiewicz
Assistant United States Attorney

Agreed and consented to:

_____
FRANK SAGGIO
Defendant

Approved by:

_____
Randi Chavis, Esq.
Counsel to Defendant

Approved by:

_____
Joseph R. Conway, Esq.
Supervising Assistant U.S. Attorney